# BEFUDDLED?

## Live the Life You Choose!

# RUSS HEDGE

Printed in the United States of America

First Printing 2020

ISBN: 978-1-09833-581-6

russ@russhedge.com

Cover design by Jordan Marsland

Photographs by Miriam Haugen of Haugen's Galleri

Editor: Joy Montgomery

*"People with their minds set on you,
   you keep completely whole,
   steady on their feet,
   because they keep at it and don't quit."*

*Isaiah 26:3 MSG*

*This book is dedicated to my beautiful wife, Leah.*
*Without her love and support for me and*
*my journey, I would not be where I am today!*

# **CONTENTS**

# *INTRODUCTION*

*"He has an air of befuddled unworldliness."*

When you are Befuddled, Merriam-Webster's Dictionary says you are unable to think clearly.

---

addle, addled, addlepated, bedeviled, befogged, bemused, bewildered, bushed, [chiefly Australian], confounded, confused, dazed, distracted, dizzy, dopey, (also dopy), fogged, mixed-up, muddleheaded, muzzy, pixilated, (also pixillated), punch-drunk, punchy, raddled, shell-shocked, silly, slaphappy, spaced-out, (or spaced), spacey, (also spacy), stunned, stupefied, zonked-out

---

### *Are YOU Befuddled?*

It means confused, living life upside down, lost in the noise of life.  So many people are walking in a haze... fuzzy and foggy... and life is still happening all around them.

Do you awake each morning and feel out of sorts and Befuddled?  No Plan or clear direction.  Are you disconnected, feeling isolated and scattered?

### *Is that you?*

We all have our days,
but it shouldn't be a way of life.

### *"Be Present!" Don't miss out!*

Are you growing and learning each day?
Remember, time is nonrefundable, so don't
waste a moment.

### *IT'S YOUR CHOICE.*

So why are you reading this book?
Is it worth your time?

### *ABSOLUTELY!*

If you need a little inspiration, encouragement,
and direction; if you want to be more positive,
if you seriously want to be a better person, and
are looking to grow personally, then this book is
for you.

### **YOU CAN LIVE THE LIFE YOU CHOOSE.**

Are you intentional, living life to its fullest and giving your presence to each moment?

What are you looking for?  What are you thinking about?

I think what we all could use is a wake-up call. We need to shake off the befuddled state that seems to permeate our culture and get some clarity in life.  We need a little more positivity. We need some more grace.  And we need a lot more kindness!

Deuteronomy chapter 30, verse 15 says ...

### *"Now listen! Today I am giving you a choice between life and death, between prosperity and disaster."*

Sounds pretty serious.  That's because it is. Your choices determine your life.

You can view it as a blessing or a curse, but you have a God-given choice, so what are you going to do with it?

### *I SAY CHOOSE LIFE!*

So, my encouragement to you today is to fight through the noise.  Be intentional.  Find purpose in the midst of the chaos.  Plan the moment. Don't live beyond now.  Failure can be built on.

Life is precious but it can be gone in an instant. So, create significance that lasts a lifetime.  The choice is yours.

### *LIVE THE LIFE YOU CHOOSE.*

You can live a more purpose driven and fulfilled life. With God's help, you can do it.  The choice is yours.  You are capable of unbelievable things!

Does your life lack clear direction?
Are you wondering what to do next in your life or business?

### *IF THAT IS YOU,*
### *THEN THIS BOOK IS FOR YOU!*

Unfortunately, many people are living in a constant befuddled state with no real "Why" in life; no driving passion to get them going in the morning!

### *IF THAT IS YOU,*
### *THEN THIS BOOK IS FOR YOU!*

Or maybe, you are just experiencing some bumps in the road and need a little encouragement and direction.

### *IF THAT IS YOU,*
### *THEN THIS BOOK IS FOR YOU!*

*BEFUDDLED?*

It's time to be intentional and live a life with purpose.  We all need a plan for the future, but we have to be present today.  You have to live life now.  Don't let it pass you by.

Life comes at you fast and furious,
and sometimes it's not all pretty.
Sometimes you'll fail.

Overcome the fear of failure and realize
you can build upon every experience in your
life, good or bad.

The truth is, if you are not failing,
you are not really trying, and you are definitely
not moving forward!

**FAILURE IS INEVITABLE, BUT THAT MEANS
SUCCESS IS JUST AROUND THE CORNER!**

So, what now?

**TIME TO READ THE BOOK!**

# 1
# *FIGHTING THROUGH THE NOISE*

In the 80s I went to college at Oregon State University (OSU).

By the way, side note, can I say the 80's was a great decade.  I loved the music, the hair (I even had some then), and the styles.  I graduated from high school in 1982, met my beautiful wife Leah in 1986, graduated college in 1987, was married in 1987, and we were expecting our daughter Kyla in 1989. Yes, it was a great decade!

## LOST IN THE NOISE

Anyway, I digress, upon entry to OSU I really had no real idea what I wanted out of life other than to graduate and get a good job.  I had no focus, no discipline, and definitely no study habits.  I was just living life by the seat of my pants, which is my nature, and I thought all was good.

I joined a fraternity, played a lot of basketball at the rec center, and partied every weekend. Slowly but surely, I lost my way.  I was definitely lost and befuddled.

It became obvious within my first year that my approach was not a winner, at least not if I wanted to stay in school.  I learned very quickly

BEFUDDLED?

that without a real plan and purpose I was easily distracted by the social side of college life.  I had no real direction.

My life was a mess.  My head was constantly pounding and the noise was unrelenting.
Oh sure, I tried to cover up my pain and confusion, but masking it with distractions only made it worse.  I was lost and needed purpose and direction.  The year was 1986, and change was coming.

There was some good.  I enjoyed the friends I made and the brotherhood.  I have always loved to connect and make friends.
In fact, to this day I have lifelong friends from my years in the fraternity house, but I was not mature enough or disciplined enough at 18 to enjoy the good without embracing the bad and getting off track.

Fraternity life turned out to be a loud distraction for me.

My life was mostly one big distraction, and I allowed it.  It was a choice I made.

But still I continued on.

I made enough changes to get my grades up a bit and stay in school, but I just couldn't find my groove.

After 4 years of college, I wasn't sure I was ever

14

going to graduate or where I was really headed! Entering my fifth year, yes, I was on the 5-year plan, God blessed me with this young lady named Leah, my beautiful wife, now, of almost 33 years. We started dating and got engaged. I suddenly had a specific purpose in life. During this time, I also found what I believe is the most important purpose, and that is a relationship with Jesus. It gave me hope and a clear direction of what I wanted out of life.

With my newfound purpose, I narrowed down my degree options and focused my studies. I changed my activity pattern and suddenly I was heading in a positive direction with an end goal in sight.

I remember the biology class I was taking at the time. I actually began to really study, not just fake it, and the first test I took was amazing. I actually knew the answers to the test. I thought, "Wow! This studying thing really works."

Not long after graduation I got a great job. Leah and I were married, and now we have a wonderful family. But it took work, focus, and intent.

It took many major events and the right people in my life to make a change. I had to focus and be intentional with my choices and direction.

**THANK GOD I DID IT, AND SO CAN YOU!**

*BEFUDDLED?*

In the next few years, I made significant changes, started making better choices and fought through the noise to clarity.

**Where are you?**

**Do you feel you are
constantly fighting through the noise?**

**Do you need clarity?**

Are you fighting your way through life trying to make sense of everything around you?  Are you stressed and discouraged with life?  Do you often wake up groggy, foggy and Befuddled? Are you lacking clear purpose and direction and wondering what in the world you're thinking; where time is going; what do I really want to do when I grow up?

**GOOD NEWS...
YOU HAVE THE POWER TO CHANGE!**

Years ago, my wife Leah and I lived and worked in Portland Oregon.  When I first began working downtown, I thought it was all cool and fun. Leah also worked downtown and we enjoyed the hustle and bustle of the city life; or so we thought.

Then our first child arrived and, suddenly, the hustle and bustle of city life became a hassle. We were overwhelmed with noise, confusion, and stress.  We needed a change.

16

We ended up moving to a smaller town and slowing down our life to focus on our family.  I was able to eventually get a job in the same city and be close to the family.

### WE EXERCISED OUR POWER OF CHOICE AND CHANGED OUR SITUATION.

So often our world swirls around us with unrelenting noise, and we get stuck in a befuddled state.  It can be a way of life if you're not careful. Life is happening so fast. It often seems like a blur.  So how do we fight through and gain some control and life balance?   By changing and making intentional good choices.

### IT IS UP TO YOU!

Change doesn't usually come easy.
In fact, it's often very difficult.

Without knowing our "Why" in life and having clarity of direction, we are subject to the trappings of the world around us.  There are so many voices vying for our attention and shouting at us to follow them.

Technology is one of the loudest voices with Social Media, Podcasts, YouTube, Google.  Who do you believe?

*BEFUDDLED?*

The information highway can be a blessing and a curse with information always at our fingertips. It also brings voices, shouting at us to do this, be this, believe this.
But, is any of it true?

With all the distractions, how do you stay focused on your real purpose and goals?  The following are three things that can help you start your day focused and on track:

1.  Start your day free of
    technology and social media

2.  Enjoy some quiet and peaceful time

3.  Recalibrate your mind to
    focus on the new day ahead

### START YOUR DAY FREE OF TECHNOLOGY AND SOCIAL MEDIA

When you start your day free of technology and social media, you give your brain a chance to focus, relax and get recharged for the new day ahead free of distractions and noise.  It is a chance to focus your thoughts and attention on something positive and center yourself and your attitude.

Meditation is a good replacement for technology and also a great way to unbefuddle your thoughts.  Whether you meditate through prayer or just solitude and quiet, it is a way free of the noise to get yourself headed your desired direction.

## *ENJOY SOME QUIET AND PEACEFUL TIME*

Enjoying peace and quiet is essential to the success you have focusing on life and all it can bring.  I love to take an early morning walk to clear my head.  It is so quiet and peaceful.  We all need that quiet moment.

When we skip this and jump right into the noise, our life can seem out of control, and noise definitely promotes the befuddled state!  We need quiet and time to hear ourselves think.

If we are at peace with God and ourselves, we can focus, meditate on positive thoughts and be real with ourselves. Then, we can see who we really are and not who we want others to see.

## *RECALIBRATE YOUR MIND TO FOCUS ON THE NEW DAY AHEAD*

Recalibration is so important to the direction we are heading.  When we recalibrate, we can focus so much better on life and the job at hand.

Getting enough rest and starting each day with time to get our bearings and get started on the right foot.  We need to recalibrate because as life continues to throw things at us, we need to hold on and stay on track to be consistent.

**START YOUR DAY FREE OF
TECHNOLOGY AND SOCIAL MEDIA**

**ENJOY SOME QUIET AND PEACEFUL TIME**

**RECALIBRATE YOUR MIND TO
FOCUS ON THE NEW DAY AHEAD**

## LIFE DIRECTION

It is a sad statement that many of us are living just to make it through the day.  We are living from paycheck to paycheck.  We are living for the weekend.

*So how are you living?*

We let life pass us by without direction or a real purpose.

**MANY OF US ARE BEFUDDLED AND
GOING NOWHERE AT TOP SPEED!**

Steven Curtis Chapman, a Contemporary Christian Artist, has a great song called "More to This Life."  The lyrics say ...

*"But there's more to this life than living and dying, more than just trying to make it through the day."*

That is such a great message and it's so true. The way we fight through and unbefuddle ourselves is to slow down, be Intentional, and focus!  Focus on why we actually get up in the morning.  That allows us to set our eyes on clear priorities for our life!

Author and motivational speaker,
Ed Mylett, says ...

### "Life happens for us not to us!"

If we truly believe that, opportunities abound and great things are possible.

If we just muddle our way through and don't really take action, we are going nowhere fast! We live life on a roller coaster.   We are up and down.  When things are good our attitude is good when things are rocky our attitude is not so good. We are being reactors not actors.

It is so important to start from a clear baseline of why we got up this morning
and what our life goals are.

We are all creatures of habit and one of the most important things is to create good habits in our life.  Experts tell us it takes somewhere between 21 and 30 days to form a new habit.

A few years ago, I created a morning habit that works great for me.

Each morning when I wake up, before I get out of bed, I tell myself three things.

First, that I am thankful for God, my beautiful wife, my family, my life, and the day to come.

Second, I tell myself I've got this.  I know that with God's help I can conquer the day.

And third, I declare it's going to be an awesome day!

These are choices I make and communicate to myself every morning and this shapes my attitude and focus for the day ahead.

Give it a try...

1.  Be thankful

2.  You've got this

3.  Today is going to be awesome!

### BE THANKFUL

Beginning with the right mindset, gets your day off to a great start.

Next, I have my morning routine of good habits that include reading, prayer, and journaling. Also, I have a workout routine each morning. This gets me started on the right foot for the day.

It's important we get started the right way because there's so many things in this life that are vying for our attention. All the noise around us is calling to us asking us to pay attention! Many times, without clear goals and direction, we are a servant to whatever comes our way.

We need to take life one small step at a time. Just one small thing after the other. Small things soon become big things. I love the quote,

**"One small positive thought in the morning can change your whole day."**

It's true, it can!

**YOU'VE GOT THIS**

We all have several profound influences in our lifetime. One of mine was my journalism professor at Oregon State, Professor Ellis. She was tough but drove you to achieve and was helpful to the end.

She taught us how to overcome writer's block, which really applies to any situation in life when you feel stuck and don't know what to do. She told us,

**"JUST DO THE NEXT DUMB THING!"**

What does that mean?

Her point was to just keep moving forward and just start writing. Just do something! This breaks you out of your funk of life whether it is writing or whatever your profession may be. I have remembered this and used it many times over the last 30+ years.  Simple yet profound.

We are what we think about, so our thoughts are so important. Especially when we're feeling befuddled.  When you're out of sorts and things aren't tracking, you need to have clear thinking. This is when a clear purpose is so important.

**IF WE HAVE PURPOSE AND
ARE PASSIONATE ABOUT WHAT WE DO,
WE CAN ACCOMPLISH AMAZING THINGS!**

***TODAY IS GOING TO BE AWESOME!***

As we discussed, the right mindset is so important.  No matter what your day throws at you, be ready and choose to look at the positive. This is how we make an awesome day. God gives us strength to make each day awesome.

Philippians 4:13 (I love this verse) says ...

**"I can do all things through Christ
who gives me strength."**

So many think everything will go perfect, but that is just not going to happen. Awesome comes when we choose to pull out the good things from each situation. We learn and grow when we keep a good positive outlook.

Today is going to be awesome is a daily choice and shapes our paradigm or filter that we look at life through.

Keep it awesome and keep it simple.

**BE THANKFUL
YOU'VE GOT THIS
TODAY IS GOING TO BE AWESOME!**

## SIMPLIFY!

Another thing that creates noise
in our life is stress.

This can happen by simply being overwhelmed. Life can get complicated!  One way to overcome this is to simplify life!

**WHEN WE SIMPLIFY LIFE,
WE REMOVE THE CLUTTER THAT CREATES
STRESS AND NOISE!**

To simplify, we need to slow down!  We need to be present and intentional in all we do.
Gary Keller, Author and founder of Keller Williams Realty, in "The One Thing" narrows it down and says to go small.  He simplifies it this way and says ...

***"What's the one thing that you can do such by
doing it, makes everything else
easier or unnecessary?"***

He breaks it all the way down to one thing. Impossible you say!  Well, how do you know until you try?  Simplicity is a great way to decrease the noise.

So, jump off the merry-go-round of life, and get in the driver's seat and take control...
it's up to you!

## HOW DO WE SIMPLIFY?

Here are four steps that have helped me.

1.  Slow Down

2.  Declutter

3.  Reduce Activity

4.  Rest and Breathe

### *SLOW DOWN*

This one is hard for me because I tend to want to do everything and I over commit.  Sometimes we have to say no and slow down.

Life moves so fast and we are often at the mercy of our schedule and our commitments. We are so activity oriented and accomplishment driven, we often lose sight of the real reason we exist.  Our "Why" gets lost in the business of life. We need to slow down, refocus, and enjoy the life we are living.  Enjoy our Journey.

## *DECLUTTER*

Remove things from your life that are unnecessary.  Get things in a more simple and clean approach.

This requires removing physical clutter as well as mental clutter. Mental clutter is one of the biggest detractors!  If we let our minds wander with negative thoughts that befuddle us, we lose control and let clutter seep in.  If however, we take control and talk to ourselves, proactively, infusing positive thoughts and giving ourselves a can-do pep talk, we take control of our minds and the situation, thus decluttering our life.

It is a choice we have to make daily, even moment by moment!

## *REDUCE ACTIVITY*

This requires making choices and slowing down enough to be intentional about the activities we are choosing to partake in.

We must be more selective in what we're doing. When we are more selective and choose our activities wisely, we don't spread ourselves so thin and keep things more simple.  This is a very important key to not overwhelming ourselves and adding stress by our own activities.  We so easily get caught up in doing things that we overdo them! We need to leave time for what's important in life, like family and friends.

### *REST AND BREATHE*

Take a step back and rest once and awhile. Recharge.  It will give you a clearer perspective.

Author and speaker Joyce Meyer says ...

> ***"I believe that the greatest gift you can give your family and the world is a healthy you."***

When you hurry through life, you don't get a clear look at what's ahead, or even what's happening at the moment.  Rest is imperative to a healthy life and it is time to put your health back as a life priority.  When you rest and breathe, you restore your strength and recalibrate your focus on life.

**SLOW DOWN**
**DECLUTTER**
**REDUCE ACTIVITY**
**REST AND BREATHE**

## MAINTAIN PERSPECTIVE!

As I write this, we are going through a crisis. Covid 19 or CoronaVirus is affecting everyone and everything around us.  Much of the country is shut down.  Many states issued a stay at home order unless you work for or need vital services or supplies.  Life has changed!

The stress and the noise have increased dramatically in many areas and the news media and social media are filled with reports of impending doom.  Now, don't get me wrong, this is a very serious situation.  I am not making light of it, but the state of confusion and befuddlement is escalating every moment and now is the time to stop, recalibrate, and rest and breathe.

**NO MATTER WHAT HAPPENS IN LIFE
IT IS ALWAYS IMPERATIVE
TO KEEP PERSPECTIVE.**

A positive perspective goes a long way to keeping a good attitude.  Attitude is everything in life because it drives our thinking and our actions.  Pastor and author Chuck Swindoll says ...

*"I am convinced that
life is 10% what happens to me
and 90% how I react to it."*

Attitude is a driving force of your life.  When you believe you can achieve things you most likely will. If you have a good attitude about your day, chances are much better you will have a good one.  When you keep a good attitude about yourself and your situation you will have a much easier time fighting through the distractions of life.

## SO, TO FIGHT THROUGH THE NOISE, WE FIRST HAVE TO CHECK OUR ATTITUDE DAILY AND MONITOR OUR PERSPECTIVE ON LIFE.

This is the beginning of peace and winning the battle over the noise!

You can do it.  You just have to purpose in your heart and be intentional.

With the right attitude and purpose, you will drive through any situation, be able to escape the noise, and persevere through any challenge!

The COVID-19 virus has plagued our world and got everybody on unequal ground.  Many are still befuddled as to what life will bring, and unsure about what the future holds.

No matter what comes our way, it is our choice how we deal with it.

I choose to hit it head on with a good attitude. I know I serve a God who has a plan, and if I put my mind to it, keeping the right mindset and choosing the right attitude, things will get better, and I will learn, grow and overcome.

And, so can you.

# 2
# *BE INTENTIONAL*

One of my earliest lessons in intentionality came while playing sports. There was definitely a specific goal. You were there to score and win the game.

I remember those times vividly!

## FOOTBALL FOCUS

It was first down and 10 in the beginning of the 4th quarter my sophomore year when the coach called my name. "Hedge, get in there!"

I played football all through school and now it was my first year in high school. I earned the starting quarterback position on the JV squad and also swung up to Varsity as a back-up.

This was the second game of the season and I had been mostly holding a clipboard and taking stats when the coach suddenly called my name. This was varsity and, honestly, I thought I was just there for support, but now I was heading into the game.

I was so excited and befuddled all at the same time that I messed up my first play of the game. The coaches signaled the plays in from the side line and my heart was beating so fast, I could hardly see. I took control of the huddle and called the play.  Unfortunately, it was the wrong play and the coaches came unglued.

Now it was time to get focused and intentional. After all, we were trying to score and secure the game.  This time I called the right play and completed a pass for 30 yards to the 10-yard line.  Talk about an adrenaline rush, I am not sure I had ever been that excited.  We went on to score and I learned to always be ready, and to keep an intentional focus when preparing and playing football.

Whether in your personal life or in business, you must be intentional in your focus and attitude. And, it works best when you begin your day with an intentionally positive outlook.

As we've discussed, this is the foundation for our approach to life, and our success.  An intentional positive start to your day is crucial. As I previously stated, I love the quote "one small positive thought in the morning can change your whole day!"  It is so true!

### ONCE YOU HAVE THE RIGHT ATTITUDE, IT SETS THE TONE FOR ALL YOU DO.

You cannot go haphazardly through life, without a real plan or destination in mind, and expect good results.  It is critically important that you are intentional about each step of your life and all you do.

Becoming unbefuddled takes effort and time. It takes consistency and practice. It's not easy, it's hard work, but the reward is great!

## FINANCIAL INTENT

Years ago, my wife and I were deep in debt and we were looking for a way out. Each month she would ask me where did all the money go? I didn't know because I had no plan and was not intentional about how we were spending. It was my job to watch over the money, and I was not doing a good job of it! Then, along came financial expert and author, Dave Ramsey. He gave a simple direction and steps to turn things around.

Number one, we had to be intentional about how we were spending our money. Also, we had to have clear goals. These included to give, save, and budget with the rest! This was not a brand new concept, but it was put in such simple terms that revolutionized my thinking. When I became more intentional about the process, a miracle happened... we paid off all our debt!

The most important detail in Dave Ramsey's plan was intent! He would say you have to "make your money behave." The point was to be intentional and plan what you were doing with your money. Then follow the plan and be consistent. Very easy steps, and very easy to understand.

So it goes with life. When we are intentional about the things we do, great things happen. We don't always reach all of our goals, but without intent there's very little chance! We don't want to go through life blindfolded, but that is what we are doing to ourselves if we have no intent and no overall objective with life.

As the old saying goes... Fail to Plan, Plan to Fail! We are going to have failures, that is just part of life, but as leadership guru and author, John Maxwell says, we have to "Fail Forward." That means to keep reaching for our life objectives and goals and picking ourselves up along the way when we don't quite reach them. Without intent, we are planning to fail because we have no goals to pursue or plans to go after.

It all starts with your attitude. Attitude drives your life. It may not be the only thing, but it is a huge factor in all that you do! When you think you can, chances are much better that you will!

Being intentional can be broken into three main areas.

1. Attitude

2. Purpose

3. Action

## ATTITUDE

We've already discussed attitude, and as I said, it is a driving force in your life. But attitude goes way beyond just a catalyst, it is the rudder to your boat. Your direction is determined by your attitude and honestly, we cannot get much at all accomplished without a good attitude. Your attitude determines how you approach life and that affects how you do life!

When you have a good attitude, you are naturally more deliberate about life. When you look for the good in things and people, you are more intentional about doing good!

Each morning, start out with the conscious purpose to make it a good day. As we discussed, it starts with a definite plan. You have to work to develop the attitude you need to be successful.

## PURPOSE

Without purpose there is no reason for achievement. Because of this, nothing really happens without knowing why you are doing what you are doing. We are going to discuss purpose more in the next chapter, but it is the motor to your boat; the energy that drives you and the reason you are able to move forward. It gives you a reason to keep going and gives you significance.

As I mentioned in the last chapter, several years ago, I began a morning routine to get my mind, body, and soul healthy. I decided to get up every morning, usually around 4am, and read my bible, journal and pray. I also exercise every day. At first, I ran every morning with my dog and did assorted exercises and arm weights. Then I had knee replacement surgery and was unable to run, so I kept up the exercises and began walking with Maddie, my beagle. Then I joined a fitness club and began riding the bike, swimming, and lifting weights. I have kept this up over 8 years. Nothing has stopped me because I was so intentional and decided that nothing was going to get in the way of my morning objective. I even keep my routine on holidays, vacations, and during the occasional head cold, 365 days a year, because I chose this with clear intent.

A morning routine like this can sometimes be difficult. Let me tell you, there have been several mornings that I did not want to get up. It's a decision I make each day intentionally, long before my alarm goes off. I decided it didn't matter how I feel, I am getting up anyway! This is the kind of intentionality needed to continue to move forward and achieve.

### ACTION

The last piece is action. Attitude and a true purpose that move you forward and give you a reason to start, and then comes action. Action is a result of the two working together. They drive your decision to make something happen. It only takes the action of one tiny step in the right direction to really propel you to greatness.

**ATTITUDE**
**PURPOSE**
**ACTION**

## #RussSelfie

Let me tell you another story.  I have been involved in sales and marketing for over 30 years.  I have always been about connecting and making friends.  As I have grown older and wiser, I have found certain activities, done intentionally, will help you connect with people much faster and help to increase your network for you and your business.

As I began to get involved in different networking groups, I discovered that people loved selfies.  I began taking them just to have fun and make people smile.  The truth is I was really horrible at taking selfies, but I just stayed with it and kept trying.

As time went on, I became a little better.  I became known as the Selfie Guy.  In fact, I took them at most events I participated in. Soon people were clambering around me and wanting me to take more of them.  I would post them on social media and tag everyone.  When I met new people, took a selfie, tagged them, and posted it, I discovered something. The next time I saw them, they remembered me and often treated me like an old friend.

It was my new found tool that built community.

## ENGAGING AND BUILDING COMMUNITY IS WHAT IT'S ALL ABOUT!

Soon after I began, I had a friend advise me to create my own hashtag... and so began the #RussSelfie. To this day I continue to take selfies, and it has expanded my influence and connections a hundred-fold. This was all because I became intentional and stayed consistent. And, I was just myself... the real me!

I really love connecting with people and selfies are a great connector and relationship builder.

Intentional connecting and networking are so important to your life and your business. True connection brings value and helps people achieve true joy in their life.

I have developed ways that help me intentionally connect throughout the years. They have come from years of experience and the wisdom of many. They are simple to say, but not so simple to do.

Here is my model for connecting.

## MAKING CONNECTIONS

There are 5 simple ways to make a connection.

1. Start (move forward)

2. Focus (be intentional)

3. Be Real and Be Friendly
(Add Value to Others)

4. Be Present (Ask Questions and Listen)

5. Be Consistent (and Repeat)

### *START*

The number one challenge people have with connecting and networking is they don't start. The first step is to get out of your Safe Place... your comfort zone... say yes and start.  In "Love Does," Bob Goff says ...

**"I used to think you had to be special for God to use you, but now I know you simply need to say yes."**

We come up with great plans and then we have so many reasons not to say yes and start.  We have to adopt a Do It Now attitude and push ahead... even if we don't feel prepared.

Life will always get in the way one way or the other, but as the old saying goes, we have time for what we make time for!

## *FOCUS*

You need to be laser focused on your connection objective, and be intentional in your approach to connecting.  If you want to meet a certain group of people, find out where they hang out.  What groups, associations, or clubs do they belong to... and then join!  Get out of your office and go where the people are!  If you don't know where to start, go to social media events and take a look!

Environment is everything in life, and when we put ourselves in the right environment to succeed, we will.

## *BE REAL AND BE FRIENDLY*

You have to be yourself and get to know people. Don't try to be someone you're not, people know when you're genuine and authentic!  Look to Add Value to others and Be Uplifting! A connection all starts with a simple greeting, authentic intent, and then takes consistent contact and intentional development of a personal relationship.  When you are truly connected and can call someone your friend, they will be motivated to be an advocate for you.  After all, Friends help Friends!

People do life and business with people they
Know, Like, and Trust!  Taking someone from
that initial contact to connecting with them
happens by giving them an opportunity to really
know you... and then they have to Like you!
Usually Likable people are Liked.  Last of all is
building their Trust!  Trustworthy people
are Trusted.

## *BE PRESENT*

Be in the moment, and listen to others.
Remember, everyone's favorite subject
is themselves.  Don't monopolize the
conversation.  Ask questions and then listen!
As John Maxwell says ...

> *"People don't care how much you know
> until they know how much you care."*

When you show you care about them and
 what they say, they will want to hang
around you more.

Most of us tend to get in a rush and hurry
through life.  Each moment is nonrefundable
and precious.  Intentionally focus on those
around you, listening and learning!

## *BE CONSISTENT*

One of the most important things in connection
is to be Consistent!  Relationships are not a one
and done.  You have to connect on a regular

and consistent basis to develop a relationship. It takes time to get to really know someone. When you are consistent, you allow time to form a true connection.

So many times, we do too many things to stay consistent in one thing! Multitasking is a great myth.  It distracts us and divides our attention!

**START (MOVE FORWARD)**
**FOCUS (BE INTENTIONAL)**
**BE REAL AND BE FRIENDLY**
**(ADD VALUE TO OTHERS)**
**BE PRESENT (ASK QUESTIONS AND LISTEN)**
**BE CONSISTENT (AND REPEAT)**

## LIFESTYLE CONNECTION

Connection is really a Lifestyle.  In order to go beyond just a contact, it takes intentional work and purpose.

***Why do you want to connect? Why do you want to be their friend?***

Ultimately, that is the test.  If you can truly answer those questions with your actions, you can gain true connection and true friendship. After all, friends are made with people that Know, Like, and Trust you.

## LOVE LEADS THE WAY

One last story about intentional relationships. Over 33 years ago I met my wife. This was the beginning of the two most important decisions of my life. The first was my relationship with Jesus.

When Leah and I first met, my life was anything but intentional. I was living by the seat of my pants and it was not pretty. I was still in college at Oregon State and I was involved in things I should not have been involved with and feeling lost.

Leah, by her living example, guided me to my intentional decision to ask Jesus into my heart and to start my relationship with Him!

That same year, Leah and I were married, after Jesus, the best decision of my life and the start of a relationship that has lasted over 33 years.

I did not choose these relationships because they were easy, because both have been hard at times, but I chose them because they were what I wanted in my life, and I made a conscious decision that no matter what happened I was not turning back or changing my mind.

Love is a choice in relationships and it is a choice you need to make long before any problems or trials arise. That is how you remain strong when they do, because in the midst, there is no decision to make.

When you make intentional life choices and set out to accomplish something; when you're consistent and make daily habits; when you purpose in your heart to go after something; your chances of success are so much greater.

# 3
# *PURPOSE IN THE MIDST OF CHAOS*

What am I doing?
Will I ever graduate?
Why am I even here?
Will anyone ever want to marry me?
I feel so lost!  These were the thoughts running through my head after 3 years in college.

## PURPOSE DRIVEN

My first senior year at Oregon State I found myself living in this befuddled state.  My mind was filled with constant chaos, and I was lost without a purpose.  I searched and searched in all the wrong places and could not find anything to fill the void that I had in my life.

When you find yourself at that place, it is not a good place to be.  The world around you says it has the answer, but with no real purpose there is no answer.  It took Jesus in my life to finally bring me purpose and remove the chaos in my head.  Oh, don't get me wrong, the chaos never really goes away, but as your perspective changes a shift comes in how you look at life.  Your attitude and your perspective override the chaos and set you on a purpose filled path.

We live in a day with lots of chaos, so do you have the right perspective?
Do you have a purpose?

*BEFUDDLED?*

Do you know where you're headed or are you too befuddled to see straight?  Are you at peace with who you are, or are you restless and filled with anxiety?

**YOU NEED A SIMPLE, SINGULAR PURPOSE TO OVERCOME THE CHAOS OF LIFE.**

I mentioned before, as I write this, we are currently going through a worldwide pandemic filled with chaos.  It is definitely the most chaos I have ever experienced in my lifetime.  Covid 19 or the CoronaVirus shut down our daily life and economies throughout the world.  Many of us quarantined in our homes, except for dealing with essential services.

Life has changed for everyone and this is a time like no other to stand strong in our purpose and find ways to accomplish life while living in almost a new reality.  It's kinda crazy!

So, this begs the question...

*Is your purpose strong enough?  Is your focus deep enough to overcome the chaos of life? When the trials come, and they will, is your purpose strong enough to keep you on track?*

Sometimes life seems unbearable.  It's times like this that we need to focus, stand strong on our purpose, and be intentionally goal driven!  This is not easy and it takes work, but most good things require an uphill climb.  We may have to struggle a bit, but in the end it's all worth it.

**YOU WILL
ENDURE AND PERSEVERE THE CHAOS
IF YOUR PURPOSE IS STRONG ENOUGH.**

If we are going to climb our mountain of chaos, we need to know where we are going.  If we know our "Why", have purpose, and are driven… we have a fighting chance.  And that is where it all starts. Romans 8:28 says …

> ***"God works all things for the good
> for those who love Him and are called
> according to His purpose."***

That means even when things aren't going so well, there still is a purpose.

With intentional purpose we have the engine that drives our meaning.  It is the force that drives us to complete our goals and to keep moving in a positive, forward direction.

So, what are some ingredients to develop purpose that can help us along the way?

Here are my four C's for purpose!

1.  Consideration

2.  Confidence

3.  Commitment

4.  Consistency

## CONSIDERATION

Intentional consideration is one of the most important avenues to a good and thought out purpose.  Life is always changing around us and we have to consider our options and really think about what we want to stand for and how we want to live.  It is this consideration that really opens up new opportunities, expanding our life and thinking based on a steadfast purpose. Without this we are just like a kite, floating in the wind.

## CONFIDENCE

We need confidence to forge ahead. It can be difficult to find confidence at times.  Without confidence we are unable to make a stand for what we truly believe.  Our purpose is the bedrock of our life.  We must have the confidence to display it.  Even when it's hard.

Fear is our enemy and is there to kill your confidence.  Fear creeps in and tries to knock down our confidence and make us question everything we do.  We all have our moments, letting fear creep in.  This is when we must stand strong in our purpose and move forward intentionally, just like we planned.

## COMMITMENT

True purpose drives commitment.  If we have purpose, whatever we do we will totally commit to it.  With commitment and follow through we demonstrate we actually believe what we stand for.

A good example is in leadership.  If you are committed to your purpose, others see it and will follow you.  A leader that has no purpose and is not committed to the path he is trying to lead others on will have no followers.  He or she will fail nine times out of ten.  John Maxwell puts it so well ...

***"He who thinks he leads, but has no followers, is only taking a walk."***

***Is that you?***

Without commitment we have no influence and can not lead.  We're just out for a walk.

## *CONSISTENCY*

And then there's Consistency.  Not only do you have to be committed once, you have to be committed over and over and be completely consistent.  There is no purpose without consistency.  If you truly believe it and are dedicated to it, you will be consistent in doing it.

It is an ongoing process and a daily decision to be consistent in all we believe.  It is not just a one and done event, but a continual and consistent process that is driven by our purpose.

Purpose is the lifeblood of significance and the fuel for your life.  It is not something that can change like the wind, but as we talked about, it needs commitment and true consistency.

*GIVE IT YOUR DAILY CONSIDERATION.*
*MOVE FORWARD WITH CONFIDENCE.*
*LET YOUR COMMITMENT BE SEEN BY ALL.*
*LET CONSISTENCY BE THE TRADEMARK OF YOUR PURPOSE!*

## SO, HOW DO WE GET THERE?

I have always tried to move forward with purpose and intentionality in my life.  I love to help people keep a positive outlook on life and be encouraged.  I also like to get involved in groups doing the same.

I am a big believer in community connection. In my business my "Why" is to encourage and help people connect and build community. This develops a strong network able to get things done.

In most communities the Chamber of Commerce is at the center of business activity so that is where I begin. With great intention and purpose, I get involved, volunteer, attend networking meetings, forum lunches and after-hours events. I get involved in committees and events, and often even become an ambassador or board member. Through this true connection begins. I am able to meet people who then introduce me to their friends and business associates, and other networking groups of interest. I then reach out and attend many of the new groups and the cycle continues.

Helping people is at the core of my "Why." I love to help, adding value to people and lifting them up. How do I do this?

I made the decision long ago to do several things to accomplish this purpose.

1.  Spread Positivity

2.  Reach Out and Encourage

3.  Seek Opportunities to Help

4.  Be Available

## SPREAD POSITIVITY

How do I spread positivity?  Every morning I start by giving myself a pep talk.  I think we all need that!  I speak positive affirmations and put myself in the right mindset immediately! It is important to talk positively to ourselves, because usually the only other thing talking in the morning is our worries and fears.

The next thing I do is my morning routine.  It is filled with God's Word, positive journaling, prayer, and exercise.

Next, I start planning how I can intentionally lift others up and who I would like to reach out to and encourage.  I post at least one positive statement on social media, and I make sure I am in the right place to start my day.

If we don't begin by getting our own attitude and mindset right, we can't help others or spread positivity.

Our positive attitude and joy is infectious and has to be the driving force for us to spread it to others.  I love the quote ...

> ***"If you want to make friends,
> you have to be friendly!"***

That is so true.  We get back what we send out. We are a mirror reflection of ourselves.  This is why I always try to live by the golden rule, treating others and I would like to be treated.

So, if you want to spread positivity today, be the person you want others to be and send out positivity.  It is definitely not a perfect science, there will be some bumps along the way, but over all you will be amazed at what you get back!

Remember, being positive doesn't mean you're always happy, it means when life gets messy and rough times come, you know there are better days ahead.

### REACH OUT AND ENCOURAGE

As I stated previously, I always look at ways I can reach out and encourage others. Our natural tendency is to look within, so we need to intentionally look outside of ourselves. It takes intentional purpose to reach out but the reward is awesome.

When I first started sending encouragement to others it is amazing how many people started encouraging me.  I didn't do it for that purpose or ask for it but what I sent out, returned to me ten-fold.

Now I have developed a definite routine of reaching out and encouraging people each morning.

As we are going through this Covid 19 crisis right now, people need encouragement more than ever.  So, I have stepped up my positivity and encouragement.  It is not only a good thing for others, it makes me feel good.

### *SEEK OPPORTUNITIES TO HELP*

When we are looking for opportunities to help others it's amazing how many come along.  If we don't have the right mindset, we will only be thinking of ourselves.  Purpose in the midst of chaos can be the driving force to direct you to seek opportunities to give and help others.

Those with clear purpose will be steadier in the midst of a storm and this helps you to find opportunities to help.

It's also a great way to raise your spirits when you help others.  We have to be intentional if we want to find opportunities.  Not often do they just fall in your lap.  You have to go get them.

### BE AVAILABLE

If we want to help others and spread positivity, we have to be available.  If we are so caught up in our own life, we have no time to help others. We are very self-focused today because of the message we get daily from the media.

It is a selfish and self-centered message. Overcome that message, be intentional, and be available.

To be available you have to make a decision. It goes beyond words. It is your actions, really being there, being present when others are in need of a help or just a positive word.  We don't realize what an impact we have on people by just being there.  When you are available and spend time with people it can change their whole day.

The most valuable commodity we have is time and when you give that away and devote your presence to others and it shows you really care.

So where does this fit into purpose in the midst of chaos?  Right smack dab in the beginning. For if your purpose is to be available to others, you help reduce the chaos and bring some purpose and calm into their life.

**SPREAD POSITIVITY**
**REACH OUT AND ENCOURAGE**
**SEEK OPPORTUNITIES TO HELP**
**BE AVAILABLE**

## GET UNSTUCK!

So many of us get stuck in the overwhelmed zone of life!

### TO FIND PURPOSE IN THE MIDST OF CHAOS WE HAVE TO GET OUT OF OUR OWN WAY.

Again, I refer to what we are currently going through with the Covid 19 Virus.  Right now, many are fearful, confused and stuck in a state of limbo.  All over the world people are overwhelmed and asking the same questions. What is my purpose... what do I do now?

What do you do when there is so much uncertainty and life seemingly comes to a screeching halt?  When things change and everything is confusing, where do you turn?

This is when your purpose, character and values really show.  They are your foundation for life. They are what drives your "Why."  Why you get out of bed each morning.  Why you do what you do. This should not change whatever the circumstance.

If you stand strong on positive purpose, character, and good values, joy and peace are available, you just have to know who you are and what you stand for.  You will find purpose in the midst of the chaos.

Remember, the most critical time for real purpose is when you're going through chaos. This cannot be overstated!  So many times, we are left flapping in the wind because we have not planned.  We have not defined our purpose. So, write it down.  Write down your values and your why.

I encourage you today to get out there, define your values and based on that define your why! When you know what you stand for your purpose will become evident!

So, fight the craziness and uncertainty and don't let yourself get overwhelmed.  Stand strong in who you really are and let your purpose, character, and values lead you to what is next.

**IF YOU LET POSITIVITY, PEACE AND JOY
RULE YOUR DAY,
YOU WILL FIND YOUR PURPOSE ...
YOU WILL FIND YOUR WAY.**

# 4
# *PLAN THE MOMENTS*

When I was young, my Mom and Dad were great planners, especially when it came to family.  They were very family focused.

Honestly, I was so blessed with great parents who cared about me, my sister Brenda, and all we were doing.  They also really cared about our whole extended family.  They planned regular family get-togethers and events.

They were so good at planning family gatherings that our house was always a very busy place. If it wasn't family, it was friends.  My Dad and Mom were expert connecters, that's where I get it from.  We had a large house with property, so it made it perfect for everyone to gather.

My Dad was the communicator and connection point for the family and would organize the event.  My Mom would then work to plan everything, including great food.  All of our gatherings included awesome food!

My Mom was an incredible cook and would put together the menu and present a huge spread of great food for everyone.  She always cooked for an army, in fact I would joke that I could invite the entire football team over unannounced and there would be enough food.

Each event would turn out spectacular because it was important to my parents to be intentional with family and plan the moments. We all knew without my parents planning, many of the gatherings would never have happened!

Often, we spend so much time looking to the future or reliving the past, we overlook the moments we have before us now. We have to be present and live now, in the present.

**THIS IS YOUR MOMENT!**
**LIVE THE LIFE YOU HAVE NOW**
**BEFORE IT IS TOO LATE.**

So many of us live for what could be, or what we hope will be, but we are not promised tomorrow, only this moment. So, what are you going to do with it!

We need to plan to act now, live now, and grow now, and tomorrow will take care of itself. It is much easier to fulfil our potential if we don't continually procrastinate the minutes and hours away waiting for just the right time. The right time is Now!

I love the saying ...

***"Good and done is better than***
***perfect and not done."***

What if we started doing one little thing at a time and letting those little things build to one big thing after the other, fulfilling our dreams for tomorrow, today.

When we truly believe today that amazing things are possible and opportunities are all around us, we suddenly can accomplish more than we ever thought was possible.

As I write this, I am approaching my 56th birthday!  Some might call that old, but I am just getting started.  I have so much life still in me and I am moving forward living each moment for all it's worth.

I have God-given goals in front of me that I will accomplish!  In fact, in the days left before my 56th birthday, I am pushing to do all I can do, as I finish out this year of my life.  I feel like I am entering a new chapter and I am so excited for all that God has for me!

I have always been the kind of guy who is positive and lives in the moment.  But, like many people, I have moments when I am losing time, looking for a better tomorrow instead of living for a better today.

Here are four things I use to live in the moment:

1. Don't Put Off Until Tomorrow What You Can Do Today

2. Dream Big with a Plan to Start Now

3. Put One Foot in Front of the Other

4. Don't Let Disappointments Be Distractions

## DON'T PUT OFF UNTIL TOMORROW WHAT YOU CAN DO TODAY

Live your life with no regrets. My beautiful wife wrote a song for a trio she sang and ministered with called "No Regrets." The lyrics are eye opening and so true. The chorus says ...

> *"Don't put off until tomorrow*
> *what you can do today,*
> *you want to live your life with no regrets."*

Whether it is with your loved ones, friends or projects with your business, don't put things off.

We humans are great procrastinators. If we can come up with a good excuse, we will put things off to tomorrow every time. Sometimes it is out of fear or maybe laziness, but whatever our excuse, we will find a way to put it off.

It is important to change our mindset to one of taking action now, for there is no time like the present. When we get in the habit of doing it now, we accomplish so much more and become much more successful.

### *DREAM BIG WITH A PLAN TO START NOW*

It is great to have big dreams, but without a plan to start now there is no purpose. This is where most people get hung up and they don't get started. You can dream all day long but, at some point, you have to make a plan and implement that plan.

Without action, dreams are just that fantasy, but by taking action, taking a risk, we can achieve great things. It just takes a start.

So, how do you do that? One step after the other. You need to be willing to risk and know that you will fail at times, but as John Maxwell would say, you just have to keep failing forward.

### *PUT ONE FOOT IN FRONT OF THE OTHER*

Forward progress now is the best way to get your momentary plans in action. We don't always feel prepared, but we just have to get the ball rolling. We need momentum. One foot after the other is the only way to go. Move forward. When we see forward progress, it builds momentum.

Often people think they have to have it all together to do anything and that could not be further from the truth. You have to start somewhere and now is the best time.

If you dream in action, moving in a positive direction and you are genuine and truthful, you are good to go. Just keep moving!

## *DON'T LET DISAPPOINTMENTS BE DISTRACTIONS*

When you let momentary disappointments distract you from your objective it is so easy to derail your plans for the moment. But, when you are grounded in your values and purpose, disappointments become new opportunities to do something better or different.

We all need something to ground us. It is what we base our character and values on. Personally, I look to God to keep me grounded and my beautiful wife to keep me on track. We all need a strong force in our lives to help us keep moving and overcome life's challenges!

Remember, others will try, but only you can derail your path. You control your choices, no matter what is going on around you. Challenges and failures will come, but if you are steadfast and grounded with a firm foundation and purpose, you will be prepared to overcome what comes your way.

Many people may try to affect your life and your decisions but that is something only you can control. Don't get off track by momentary setbacks or others distracting you.  Keep moving forward and you can do great things.

**DON'T PUT OFF UNTIL TOMORROW
WHAT YOU CAN DO TODAY
DREAM BIG WITH A PLAN TO START NOW
PUT ONE FOOT IN FRONT OF THE OTHER
DON'T LET DISAPPOINTMENTS
BE DISTRACTIONS**

## HOW DO WE RESTORE BALANCE?

Life without some balance is a catastrophe waiting to happen!  I realize we will not ever be able to accomplish perfect balance because things are always changing.  We do however need to create a somewhat level playing field so our life doesn't tip over on us.

This is a life challenge we can achieve, but only when we pay attention and restore the proper weight to our most important life priorities.

Priority balance is necessary or you will live a life full of stress and struggle instead of moving forward and making positive progress.

The following are four ways you can help to restore balance to your life...

1. Use the right scale

2. Properly weight priorities based on your values

3. Remove items tipping your scale the wrong way

4. Be consistent in your balancing act

### USE THE RIGHT SCALE

If you are not using the proper scale to weigh your life priorities, you will constantly be out of balance. This is a challenge with many people who look to compare themselves to others. You are your own individual and you will never have balance if you're judging yourself off of what others achieve or have.

Using the right scale, based on your values and plans will keep you on track and balanced in all you do. You are your own wonderfully talented person, so go live your life not someone else's.

### PROPERLY WEIGHT PRIORITIES

Balance involves not only using the right scale, but also a firm foundation on values and character. When you know what you stand for it's a lot easier to stand and stay balanced!

Situations in life often draw you into new surroundings with new people that can often seem stressful and unbalancing.  But if you are grounded and know what you stand for it's always easier to stay balanced.

Life is full of your choices every day, so remember they are your choices and you can stay balanced by properly weighing your priorities.  When you do this, you will achieve a much better balance and be able to live the life you choose.

### REMOVE ITEMS TIPPING YOUR SCALE

You can often get weighed down with the wrong situations or people in your life that will tip your scale the wrong way.  These situations have to be dealt with and often removed from your life to stay balanced.

The choices of who you associate with and what situations you put yourself in are up to you.  Remember, you have the power to control what you choose, so remove those items that get you off track.

### BE CONSISTENT IN YOUR BALANCING ACT

Finally, you have to be consistent in what you believe to stay balanced.  When you are consistent in your priorities, using the right scale, properly weighing your priorities based on your values, and removing items tipping your scale the wrong way, it is a lot easier to achieve your balancing act.

Consistency is really the secret to keeping your life balanced and building good forward momentum. Keep with it and your balancing act will be so much easier.

So, stay in the moment and live your plan today. Life is so precious. We don't want to lose out on all the great opportunities before us. When you plan your moments and apply action, life is really a wonderful place to live!

**USE THE RIGHT SCALE
PROPERLY WEIGHT PRIORITIES
REMOVE ITEMS TIPPING YOUR SCALE
BE CONSISTENT IN YOUR BALANCING ACT**

## VALUE ADDED

You have great value to add to your life and to others.  It is important that each day you remind yourself of that fact and make choices that move you in a positive direction!

Restoring your balance and living your plan today is your secret to success.  Because success truly is based on significance and significance takes planning.  So, plan the moments and...

**GO LIVE TODAY!**

# 5
# *DON'T LIVE BEYOND NOW*

Don't live beyond now.  Sounds pretty simple, so why aren't you doing it?

## DREAM HOME

My wife Leah and I always wanted to own our own home.  In fact, back in the early 90's we used to dream about our first home, so much so, when we found a model home in our area we really liked, we would visit it often, hang out, and dream.

The model home was usually open during the day for people to take a look.  We'd go in, on more than one occasion and pretend we lived there.  We acted like it was our home.  It was a wonderful dream, but with our finances, as a newly married couple, it seemed so far.  But that didn't stop us from dreaming.

We even talked with a builder at one point but because of finances, it seemed impossible.  Our problem was, we were not living in the moment, we were only dreaming.  Being present and in the moment, you find a way, and throw caution to the wind.  You just do it.

We were living in the Portland area and houses, in general, were more than we could afford at the time.  We wanted our own home but just didn't know how to get it.

One day, I was talking to my oldest brother-in-law, Doug.  Doug was the big brother I never had and he had some great advice.  He said "now is the time."  He told me we would need to make some adjustments to our plan and it could be a reality now.  We had to make a way for it to work.  We had to live in the now not just in the dream.

That is exactly what we did.  We moved out of our duplex and moved in with Leah's Grandma for about 6 months.  She allowed us to live there free of charge while we searched for a house.  We concentrated on real estate in the Salem area, which was much less expensive and closer to our budget.  We took immediate action by maintaining a strict budget, saving our money, getting pre-approved for a house, and consulting with a real estate agent.

Six months later, we moved into our first home just before our daughter's second birthday.  It was a great day because it was the culmination of all our hard work.

What if we had only kept dreaming and didn't take action?  It may have been years before we bought our first home.

Too often we live only hoping or idealizing about the future.  We find ourselves stuck in the past, imagining what used to be and miss what is right before us.  Don't Live Beyond Now!  Now is all we truly have.  God has not promised us tomorrow on this earth, so we must enjoy our journey today.

Every moment of life is precious.  We easily miss out because we are living beyond this moment.  We should love what we do right now.

The late, great Kobe Bryant said ...

> **"You should always love what you do and then work hard and get after it!"**

What great advice we should all aspire to.  While it is important to plan ahead and dream for the future, we must also focus on the present and what we love to do.  If we don't get after it and we don't take action, this moment will pass and we will miss out.

I love the quote ...

> **"Time is nonrefundable."**

I believe the author of that quote is unknown, but he or she was on to something.  We can not get back the time that goes rushing by, and it goes so fast!

I remember the first time I was told I better enjoy my kids because the time would go so fast, and I would respond, "yeah I know."  Well, the truth is, I had no idea how quickly.  It seems like just yesterday.  I blinked and now my kids are 30 and 27.  Wow, it really did go fast.

That is why I am committed to not live beyond now. I want to soak in every moment God gives me on this earth. I know there will come a day when it is all over, but until then, I am going to enjoy all I'm given.

We need to focus on the time we have and take advantage of the opportunities God has given us. There is so much possibility today. When you are feeling out of sorts and time seems to be working against you, remember these four things:

1.  Only now is guaranteed.

2.  Action is required.

3.  Take one step at a time.

4.  There is a bigger plan.

### ONLY NOW IS GUARANTEED

I have a wonderful father-in-law, Ben. His favorite saying, when I talk about my plans for the future is, "Lord willing." His point is, only the Lord really knows our future, and it is not guaranteed. We only have the here and now, so let's take care of it.

Every moment, starting as soon as we wake up, is important. We need to make the most of the life we are given. There is so much opportunity and possibility all around us. So many people are in need and wanting attention.  If we're not watching and listening, we will miss out.

I can't emphasize it enough, enjoying the journey of our life is a one-time deal!  We don't get do overs.

As I said earlier, this was never more evident to me that when our children were growing up.  Everyone told us it would go so fast, but you never really know until it's over and their childhood is gone.  The time and effort we put into our family is so important and it makes a lifelong impact.

I remember when our kids, Kyla and Connor, were young we recognized they were extremely talented musically.  We dedicated time and effort to music.  In church they played and sang on the worship team.  In school they participated in choir and band.  My son had his own band that played gigs and recorded music. Both kids competed nationally in music festivals because of their talent and because of their discipline.  They developed their God-given skills because they spent time, daily, on what they loved.

They are adults now, and through their music, they have touched thousands of people. Both of them have played and sang before large groups in concerts and conferences, but it is because they spent time developing their talents instead of only dreaming about

possibilities.  They lived in the now.
Their effort paid off; they have enjoyed a
musical journey that still continues today.  Our
daughter Kyla, graduated with a Bachelor's
Degree in Music Ministry and has led worship
throughout the world.  Our son, Connor is a
professional musician, writing and producing
music.  He still travels throughout the country
playing, singing and sharing his music.

So, purpose today to make the most of every
moment.  Make it your goal to positively affect
people and achieve what God has laid out for
you.  It's a choice you make daily, and it's really
up to you!

### ACTION IS REQUIRED

Once you have made the choice to live in the
present, action is required.  A dream and a plan
without action don't get you very far.

Forward momentum is necessary.  Don't let
fear of the unknown or making mistakes hold
you back.  You will be scared and you will make
mistakes, but that's how you learn.

If we had stopped at our dream for a house,
never made the appropriate adjustments, and
never took action, we may still be living in a
rental to this day.

Look around you and see how many people are caught in a life they never wanted. They are saying some day. They don't feel ready, so they just sit and do nothing.

Be assured it takes time, and it takes action. But, just one foot in front of the other is all you need. Take one step at a time.

### TAKE ONE STEP AT A TIME

Life doesn't happen all at once, it happens bit by bit, step by step. As we keep moving forward little by little things start to happen now. This is called progress.

Sometimes things may seem to change in leaps and bounds, but it's usually a slow process that we will miss if we're not paying attention. How many times have you said, "wow, it all happened so fast."

It really is about being present. This is an issue I deal with daily. I am so busy doing so many things that I often overlook being present in the moment, not really listening to my wife or listening to my friends or others around me. This is critical to taking the right steps in life.

In taking our life steps we can do the walking, or we can let ourselves be walked.

### THERE IS A BIGGER PLAN

What happens in this life is much bigger than us. I believe it is in God's hands and we are just along for the ride. However, this doesn't mean we don't do anything, just sit back and let God take care of everything. It means we recognize there is something bigger than us and it's not all about us.

## THAT CAN BE HARD FOR ME!

No matter what you believe, the reality is that life is much bigger than just us! We must realize that everything we do affects others and we are affected by what others do around us.

My wife Leah works at an elementary school. Recently, she told me how difficult it is to create a master schedule for the school because there are so many people involved and so many moving parts. In order to put together a working schedule they have to look at the big picture, otherwise it would create chaos.

We need to look at the big picture and develop an outward approach. This helps us avoid being so inwardly focused. It is the development of the habits of giving and helping that will achieve this purpose. As we look to others, the bigger plan and life has a way of taking care of us.

**ONLY NOW IS GUARANTEED.**
**ACTION IS REQUIRED.**
**TAKE ONE STEP AT A TIME.**
**THERE IS A BIGGER PLAN.**

## THE BIGGER PLAN

Our environment dictates the information going into our brain, and as we discussed at the beginning, there is a lot of information thrown at us every moment of every day.

When we develop big picture thinking, we realize that there is so much more to this life.  We start taking a better look at others' perspectives.  We make choices based on how it affects others, and not just ourselves.

For example, I grew up playing sports and learned a lot about teamwork.  While I was trying to see how many points I could score, or how I looked on the court or field, my coach's objective was to help the team win.  I was narrow in my thinking, while my coach had the big picture in mind.  He was looking out for the whole team, not just me.

As I grew into young adulthood, I was able to be on the coaching end of sports and it gave me a whole new perspective.  Now I was the one concerned about the whole team effort and the goal of winning as a collective unit.

## COACHING LESSONS

My first experience coaching came in my last couple years at Oregon State. One of my friends and roommates partnered up with me and we volunteered to coach football and basketball at an elementary school. It was a lot of work, but it was so much fun!

We were blessed with some good athletes and we won a lot of games. The boys were really sharp too, so we were able, at the 4th and 5th grade level, to accomplish quite a bit.

Sometimes I would laugh. In football, some coaches were just trying to teach their boys the very basics while we were running rather complicated schemes for elementary school. We were signaling in plays from the sideline, running motion on offense, and stunts on defense. At times, the other teams didn't know what even hit them. We just figured, why not try it now and see how much the boys absorbed, and we were met with amazing results.

It was an enjoyable first coaching experience, but it also taught me the importance of every member on the team. They had to work together. Selfishness didn't get us anywhere.

It is important to be like a coach with big picture thinking. Taking in all that this life entails.

It really is about the effect we have on others and not just ourselves.

Big picture thinking considers others and realizes that we don't live in a bubble. Everything we do affects others.

When we grow into this type of thinking, it changes us.  It becomes our paradigm of life and how we look at things.  We are no longer concerned solely about ourselves, but we are thinking about others.

When you live this way, it is incredible how much more you get accomplished.
What does it take?  How do you live now and not beyond today?

Well, it takes intentionality and practice.  It doesn't just happen, because we are wired to dwell on the past or just cross our fingers and hope it will be better in the future.

Here are 4 things that have really helped me:

1.  Be Passionate

2.  Be Now Driven

3.  Find New Ways to Engage Now

4.  Live Today

## BE PASSIONATE

What are you really passionate about?  Do it!
Be passionate now!  Don't wait for someday to
come.  Get going.  Let your passions drive your
journey today and create new
experiences tomorrow.

I believe passion is what God put inside each
one of us and when your passions are active,
great things happen.  Your passions come from
your "Why" and drive your "How."

## BE NOW DRIVEN

Turn your passion into drive today.  Let now
be the platform for your accomplishment.  You
create significance in your life by moving in your
passion positively and you affect yourself and
others in a positive way.

When you are now driven amazing things
happen because you make them happen.
When it's really your passion, it is hard to put it
off because it is rooted so deeply inside of you.

## FIND NEW WAYS TO ENGAGE NOW

Be creative.  Find new ways now to engage your
brain and your body to action.  When you let
yourself be creative it fuels your passion and
desire to drive ahead and engage now.

The beautiful thing about passion is it breeds creativity and helps new ideas to flow.  So, let the creative juices flow.

## *LIVE TODAY*

Today is your day, so live it!  Why only dream about tomorrow?  Make today your vision and make possibilities come true.  Only you can make that choice so why not do it.

There are once-in-a-lifetime choices you have before you now and the decisions you make today will affect you for the rest of your life.  Oh, and by the way, not deciding and lack of action are decisions.

### SO, DON'T LIVE BEYOND NOW.

Remember, only now is guaranteed.  Action is required.  Just take one step at a time.
There is a bigger plan.

You will enjoy the results of living this way and you will find a greater reward as you passionately live for others.

### BE PASSIONATE.
### BE NOW DRIVEN.
### FIND NEW WAYS TO ENGAGE NOW.
### LIVE TODAY.

# 6
## *FAILURE CAN BE BUILT UPON*

New York Times Best Selling Author Bob Goff, in his book Love Does, writes ...

*"Failure is just part of the process, and it's not just okay; it's better than okay. God doesn't want failure to shut us down. God didn't make it a three-strikes-and-you're-out sort of thing."*

It was my freshman year at Oregon State. I was so excited. I had a full load of classes and I was ready to take on the world. What I didn't realize now is that I actually had to take action and do something. I had to work, study, and achieve, all on my own.

You see, I was a good kid in high school, which basically meant I was guaranteed at least a B with very minimal work. I loved high school, but it didn't really prepare me for the next step, and I was about to learn a lesson on failure.

## ON MY OWN

In the fall of 1982, I took the Oregon State University (OSU) campus by storm. I began connecting and making tons of friends, as well as reconnecting with old friends who were also attending OSU. If there was a grade given for connecting, I would have definitely gotten an A.

Everything started great. How hard could it be, right? I had passed through High School in the top 10% of my class, earned several awards, and finished with about a 3.7 grade point average.

Now I was on my own. No parents to look after me and no teachers holding my hand and giving me the benefit of the doubt because I was a good kid.

The first few weeks were great, and then the school work began to pile up and I was too busy majoring in basketball and socializing with friends.

It came time for midterms and I was not ready. I failed miserably! In two of my six classes I received an F. I had never failed a test before. I thought I could make it up, but things just got harder and worse, and the fact that I would rather go play basketball than study was a definite problem.

Well finals time came and my roommate and I were studying one night when I realized I was not going to pass my economics or my math class. I was living in a befuddled state. I had taken sophomore level courses and I should have stayed at the freshman level.

I was feeling it was too late at this point, so instead of studying, my roommate and I drove home to help our families decorate for Christmas. I didn't know what else to do. It was a good stress relief, but it didn't help the outcome of my finals the following day.

I failed miserably on both my economics and math finals and thus failed both classes. In economics it was so bad, at the end of the term I didn't even know what economics really was. I know, I know, I was a horrible student.

I received a 1.79 GPA for my first term and was immediately on academic probation.

Huge failure... Huge problem!

Now it was time to shape up, at least a little bit, and pass some classes. I learned more about the university system and found I had the ability to withdraw from classes if I got in over my head. I could also retake classes I failed for a new grade, which I would ultimately do.

Well, the good news came my second term. I must have learned something from my mistakes and failure. I improved to a 3.0. I still had a long way to go and lots of ups and downs but, in the end, I learned a lot.

Ultimately, I built upon my failures and graduated with my Bachelors of Science in Communications with almost a 3.0.

Yep, a B.S in Speech Communications. That explains a lot!

In the end it was a lot of work, but I learned and grew into a much better version of me.

## FAILING

One of the most important lessons I have learned is that life happens, and then what matters most is what we do with it. Failure is something we all encounter! In fact, it is necessary. In the end, we are all responsible for our own outcome. It is ultimately on us.

John Maxwell says in his book called *Failing Forward* ...

> ***"Failure is simply a price we pay to achieve success."***

When we are willing to risk and try new things, we are going to fail no matter how good we are.

Failure often puts individuals into a befuddled state. They are so dazed and confused that they stop trying. And so many are afraid to fail they never really try. They don't take a risk. With no risk there is seldom accomplishment.

What they don't realize is that ...

### FAILURE CAN BE BUILT UPON!

Many years ago, when I was first learning to ski, I learned a very valuable lesson that has stuck with me over the years. I had a friend that invited me and began by teaching me the basics.  He told me that I was going to fall and that was ok.  I said, that is not ok with me, I don't want to fall!  But he continued, nobody wants to fall or fail, but if you're not falling, you're not learning.

I had to think about that for a while, but then I realized he was right.  There was no way to improve beyond the bunny slope if I was not willing to take risks.  So, I did and, by the end of the first day, I was already skiing more difficult slopes.  And yes, I fell a lot!

When we take risks and learn to overcome failure, we set ourselves up for constant improvement. One step at a time. It doesn't happen overnight but when we keep putting ourselves out there and trying, we will definitely improve.

## THOUGHT OVER FAILURE

A positive mindset is so important.

Philippians 4:8 in the Bible says ...

> *"Fix your thoughts on what is true, and honorable, and right, and pure, and lovely, and admirable."*

Don't let your thoughts about life get you off track.  Think of good and positive things!  Don't get caught up in what happens, but learn to adapt and to work within the situations we are given.  Often that means stepping out of our comfort zone, engaging our brain, and trying something new!

It is a state of mind.  A mindset of continuing on in spite of your current circumstances.

Often, we are in a situation in life and we are blinded by our own perception and paradigm of life.  We all have blind spots and they can keep us from achieving all that's before us.

One way to overcome blind spots and our own faulty perception is to step out of ourselves and take a look from a new perspective. This usually takes someone else's help.  An outside person looking in. It doesn't necessarily mean there is anything wrong with us, it may mean we are just not seeing the whole picture.  That is why mentors are so important.

There have been several times in my life when this has been the case.  I have been blessed with the perspective of family and friends that have helped me overcome my blind spots and improve myself through the failures.

Even as I write this, I am learning from a situation I am currently going through. Situations can sometimes be painful and hard, but we have to stand strong in our values and beliefs and do what we know to be consistent with our character, we will more often than not come out on top. It is something we all have to go through and that is how we grow.

Romans 5:4 says that ...

**"Endurance develops strength of character."**

Enduring the struggle builds character and if we are willing to learn from it, it teaches us new lessons.

It is similar to physically working out and building strength and muscle. It is always hard and a struggle, but in the end the benefits are great. Your muscles grow and you get your body in great shape.

I remember the workouts for football in high school. Weekly we would have regular weight lifting workouts and they were painful. Often, I didn't think I could do it and I wondered why I was doing it, but I stayed with my commitment. Because I didn't quit and because of the ongoing workouts, I grew stronger and gained muscle. I became better because I endured the pain and persevered.

We have to look to the end results and reward when we are going through the pain. It is what is on the other side that keeps us going. When we can see beyond our current circumstance, we can achieve great things.

When you persevere through struggle, you will find you are rewarded.  Just like the struggle of training and practicing football made us ready for the games.  Games were an awesome reward after the pain of the preparation and practice.

You can also go through a similar struggle in dating.  You are looking for the right match and it often takes trial and error.  There are mountain top moments and then break ups and valleys that are very painful, but in the end the results can be awesome.  Finding a life-long partner through the process is the wonderful benefit.

Failure in our life journey is inevitable, but if you allow yourself to learn from it, you will be better on the other side.

Here are 3 things that have helped me overcome failure along the way.

1.  Face fear

2.  Do it Now

3.  Learn and Grow

### FACE FEAR

Fear is the #1 thing that holds us back.  The bible tells us 365 times not to fear.  I think God was trying to make a point.  This doesn't mean fear is going to magically disappear.  We are human after all.  If we are not supposed to fear, then what do we do?

You have to be willing to face your fears, start and try something new.

We are all going to be fearful at times, but if you don't get going you will never overcome the fear.  When you are willing and put your willingness into action, it will get you going in the right direction.

So many people let their fear overwhelm them and they are never willing to step out and take a chance.

You will always have fear in your life, but you can overcome with God's help and a willingness to try!

It is like the first time you ride a bike.  You are afraid of falling and that can hold you back, but when you work to overcome your fear, keep trying in spite of falling and skinning your knees, you conquer the bike and learn to ride.  It is an exhilarating experience.

## DO IT NOW

My Dad was a man of action. I believe that is where I get my approach to life. He always seemed to have a plan. He had a heart to help others and he was always busy doing something. He did not sit back and wait for people to come to him. He went to them.

He would find a project that needed done and instead of spending all day figuring out how to do it, he would just jump in and start working. And he was a very hard worker.

Like my Dad, I believe you have to jump in with both feet and just do it now. Throw caution to the wind and make things happen. Sometimes it may even seem a little crazy.

This reminds me of the Polar Bear Club at YMCA camp when I was a kid. To be a member of the club, you had to wake up early each morning and jump into freezing cold water. The only way I could make this happen was to not overthink it and worry, but just do it. It was cold and shocking, but when I did it, I realized it could actually be done and it didn't kill me. It was actually an exhilarating experience.

I have a do it now mentality to this day that has helped me in my life and my business. If it is possible and financially feasible I do it right away. I feel that if I put it off it won't get done. With that in mind I continue to **do it now!**

### LEARN AND GROW

Failure can definitely be built upon and as I said earlier, you can learn and grow from it. It is what you learn from each experience and failure that helps you to grow. Don't just accept the status quo but reach out and try new things. Be adventurous.

Simon Sinek says that ...

> ***"Failure is when you accept the lot you were given."***

If you just accept your condition, advancement and achievement are nearly impossible. If you continue to learn and grow you will be significant and thus successful.

Thomas Edison was reported to be too dumb to learn by his teachers and he failed 1000 times before successfully creating the light bulb. Unlikely you have failed 1000 times at something, so if Thomas can do it, so can you!

Learn and grow and build on the failures along the way. Remember, just because you fail at a task doesn't make you a failure as a person.

John Maxwell says ...

> ***"Without failure there is no achievement."***

Instead of worrying and fretting about failure, turn your failures into stepping stones for achievement. Everything happens for a reason and your failures can be built upon.

***FACE FEAR***
***DO IT NOW***
***LEARN AND GROW***

## LEARNING

When we step back and really look at what happens to us, we can learn from any situation, good or bad.

**FAILURE SHOULD BE**
**THE STEPPING STONES OF YOUR LIFE.**

There often will be pain along our journey but in the end, if we keep stepping forward, we will learn and grow.  It is one stepping stone at a time and the forward progress will help you gain the momentum you need to succeed. Failure is not final. It is part of your journey. Stack one experience upon the other and before you know it you are gaining ground.

**THIS IS WHERE YOUR FAILURES**
**BECOME STEPPING STONES.**

Each experience can teach us an incredible lesson and we can learn and grow, expanding our knowledge, and making us a better person.

Without the struggle, our beauty cannot emerge.  Much like the butterfly.  If the caterpillar is not allowed to struggle and grow into a butterfly, and then the butterfly is not allowed to fight its way out of the cocoon, it will not be strong enough to fly.

Just like the butterfly, you were meant to fly.  Maybe not literally, but fly as in take action and soar.  If you make it a habit of persevering and standing strong in the midst of challenges, you will become much stronger and achieve more than the average person.

You were meant to encounter struggle and failure.  It is the normal course of life.  If things were always easy, you wouldn't work to learn and improve. You might grow lazy and just waste away.

So, what is the answer to this challenge?

**TAKE EACH CHALLENGE IN LIFE,
VIEW IT AS AN OPPORTUNITY,
AND LEARN, LEARN, LEARN!**

We are all life-long learners.  Life is really a continuous educational process.  When we choose to learn, grow, and turn our failures into stepping stones, we can make amazing things happen.

Don't give up!  When you stick with it, learn from each situation, especially your failures, you will be a better person for it.  You will have the opportunity to achieve more and you will slowly build the life you've dreamed of.  But it takes effort.  It doesn't just happen.

Remember, failure can be built upon, and you are just the one to do it!  So, keep a positive attitude, learn from your failures, and go make it a great life!

# 7
# *GONE IN AN INSTANT*

Life is all about perspective.

## MIRACLE

It was July 9th, 1983. I was 19 years old.  It was a day like any other.  I had completed my first year at Oregon State University and was home for the summer.  My Dad was starting a Satellite TV business and I was helping him out.  It was a beautiful day at our home in Oregon City, Oregon.

I had spent most of my growing years at this home.  We had 5 wooded acres on a bluff with a beautiful view.  My Dad and I were installing our first satellite dish at our home and learning how it all worked.

The installation was not going well as we were very inexperienced.  We had a disagreement and we were both frustrated.  There was tension in the air.

My Dad and I had a great relationship but this happened occasionally because I always wanted to move at a lightning pace and my Dad was slow and steady.  Things were not working well on this day, and we both needed some space.

I had to get away for a bit to cool down, so I told my Dad I was going to a small golf course a few miles from my house to clear my head.

It was a great day for golf, and I loved this little par 3 golf course. I had a relaxing round golfing and I loaded up my clubs to head back home. That is the last thing I remember.

The rest of this story was pieced together for me over many months by several sources.

As I drove away from the golf course, I approached a highway. There was a slight ridge with railroad tracks just before it dropped to the stop sign at the entrance to the highway. Eye witnesses say I was going about the speed limit, but made no attempts to stop and flew right through the stop sign and onto the highway where my Toyota Celica was hit by a pick-up truck going about 60 miles an hour.

The Toyota Celica I was driving I had just purchased just 7 days earlier. It was used but it was new to me. Just like that, it was gone in an instant. I was not far behind.

I'm sure I was beyond befuddled at that point. Eye witnesses said it launched me to the other side of the highway and I ended up against a small tree on a church property. God was definitely looking after me.

I was told I was in a semi-conscious state, fighting for my life, but I have no memory of the event even to this day.  As I write this book, I am almost 56.  In one of the cars behind me was a nurse who called 911.  She assessed the situation and did not think I would survive an ambulance ride to the hospital so they called Lifelight.

Eyewitness accounts said they couldn't believe that anyone in my Celica could survive the accident, but God had other plans.  The impact was so great that the pick-up truck and its canopy separated and flipped over.  The driver and his wife were taken to the hospital and released the same day, thankfully, with mostly bumps and bruises.

I, on the other hand, was in need of immediate life-saving help.  When the emergency vehicles arrived, they used the Jaws of Life to get me out of my car.  My entire car had collapsed around me and had crushed my upper torso.

They extracted me from the vehicle and landed the Lifelight Helicopter in the middle of the highway.  I was flown to Emanuel Hospital in Portland where they had a trauma team standing by.

I had severe head trauma and swelling of the brain.  I had broken several ribs, both collar bones, and my jaw in 3 places.  A rib had punctured one of my lungs and they both collapsed.  Hot water from the radiator had scalded my feet and I was left with 3rd degree burns on both.

After hours in surgery I was in critical condition and they were uncertain if I would survive. During all of this, my parents received the call that no parent ever wants to get about their child.  They were told I had been in a horrible accident and was in critical condition.

My parents and sister had to make the 40-minute drive from Oregon City to Portland knowing that at any moment I could be gone.

It was something that no family should have to go through but mine did.  It was painful but sometimes life is that way.

Well, my story has a good ending.  I survived. About three weeks after the accident I was released from the hospital for outpatient treatment and therapy.  And in September of that same year, I was back at Oregon State for fall term.

It was the amazing hand of God and a bunch of fine medical professionals that saved my life. It was my loving family that supported me and helped me get back on my feet.  My story ended well.

**MY LIFE COULD HAVE BEEN
GONE IN AN INSTANT.**

## YOUR PERSPECTIVE

This brings us back to perspective.

### *What is your perspective?*

What we perceive around us and how we approach each situation we encounter and it builds our life paradigm.

Take a look at your life, appreciate what you have because it could be gone in an instant. Like I mentioned earlier, you are not guaranteed beyond now and you should live like today is all you have.  Be joyful and share that joy with your circle of influence.

I am so grateful for my life and the 37 years I have had since the accident.  When you live a miracle, it gives you a whole new perspective on life.  You count your blessings more closely and you appreciate all the good things you have. When you are stuck in a befuddled state, there is no clarity or appreciation for life.

This befuddled state that so many are plagued with can take you out of the game.  It is a huge life distraction and gets our eyes off the prize. Remember how blessed you really are.

Living in the United States my struggles do not compare to the suffering some people endure in other parts of the world.  Often, my befuddled state comes from missing a morning

Latte', not having service from my smartphone, staying up too late, watching movies, and not getting enough sleep.

The Covid 19 crisis brought us the pain and suffering of disease. It brought on economic stresses with people losing their jobs and many, their businesses.

Most of us are so blessed and live lives of relative comfort. But all we have could be gone in an instant.

Psalms 15 says ...

> **"He knows our lives are short,**
> **that they are like grass."**

We are only here for a season and we have to appreciate every moment we are given.

In our most befuddled state, we always have a choice to change and make things better. We can snap out of it and learn an appreciation for the little things in life.

True perspective often tells us that things aren't really so bad after all. We are just in need of a tune-up, although I know it doesn't seem like that when we are in the middle of pain or a challenging situation.

## MY PERSPECTIVE

In July 1983, my Toyota Celica was gone in an instant.  My summer break was gone in an instant.  My life and my parents' life, as we knew it, for the couple months after my accident were gone in an instant, but my life was spared by the grace of God.

So, my perspective shifts and all the everyday worries and befuddlement seems like a trifle compared to what was and what could have been.

This is why we need to reexamine our lives daily when we are feeling befuddled and realize how blessed we really are.  Often with a tune up on our attitude and outlook we can hit life head on.  By making some changes we can create a significance that we never realized we had.

Buried deep inside of us, God has a plan to remove our state of befuddlement.

Not everyone comes out of their challenges in life the same.  I was able to walk away from my accident with a little work and persistence, but I had a friend who was not so fortunate.

## BILL'S PERSPECTIVE

Bill had a car accident about the same time I did.  We ended up in the same hospital recovering. At one point they took me in to visit him.  As I said, he was not able to walk away from his accident.  He lived, but he was paralyzed from the waist down.  His life walking was gone in an instant.  Things changed drastically for him and it was then that he had to make a choice.

*You know what he chose?*

He chose to make something out of his life after his accident.  In spite of his circumstance, he chose to do something positive.  His ability to walk may have been gone in and instant, but not his life.  After some time in the hospital and some life adjustments, Bill set out to make his life count.

### IT IS ALL PERSPECTIVE.

Bill didn't live his life depressed or in a constant befuddled state because of his circumstances, he lived the life he chose.  I am sure it was very hard at times.  I can only imagine what he must have gone through during that time.  It was hard enough for me, but he chose the positive road.  He chose to do all he could in spite of what had happened.

## HE CHOSE A GOOD PERSPECTIVE.

Bill did incredible things with his life and to this day lives with his wife in Oregon. He has been productive and, from all appearances, is a happy man. I know he has the joy of the Lord and that is definitely his strength.

Today you have that same choice. Every moment of every day we can live in a fog and befuddled, or we can choose to rise above and live our best life now.

Our attitude is up to us and so is our outlook. It's really as simple as that.

Oh, I know it isn't easy, but it is doable. And You Can break out and do it if you really set your mind to it.

## MINDSET, MINDSET, MINDSET!

This is the key, and this is the same in your personal life or business.

I realize I do not know your situation, only you and God know that, but I do know that how you look at things, your mindset or paradigm, are what shape where you are going from here.

So, what are you going to choose to do today? Are you going to choose a significant life in spite of what you are going through, or are you going to let your circumstances control you!

## LIFE PERSPECTIVE

I lost my Dad a couple of years ago to lung cancer and dementia. It all happened in a very short period of time. I had moved him and my Mom into an independent senior living community to enjoy their final years. My Dad had beat lung cancer, or so we thought, and my Mom was in the early stages of Alzheimer's.

When they moved in, I thought it would be great for them. They had a nice apartment off a beautiful courtyard and a restaurant style dining room with all meals included. Honestly, I was ready to move in. But oh! How things changed quickly.

Not long after the move, we discovered Dad's cancer had returned and he was showing signs of dementia. I was really in denial, but my beautiful wife Leah kept me on track and only a couple of months after the move my Dad was in hospice.

The final day of his life, things were not good and he was in a lot of pain. We had hospice and a caregiver hired and onsite to help. I had stayed the night in their apartment the night before and things were not looking good. I was so glad to have the support of the hospice nurse and the caregiver. I also had my wife and many others praying.

They finally got the pain under control later that evening. I went home for a couple of hours to get some rest. My Dad passed away and went to be with Jesus just after midnight - about 2 hours after I left. He was gone in an instant.

## THE LEGACY

I could have been bitter and frustrated with life. I could have been mad at God for taking for my mentor, the man who was the foundation of my life, but I chose to focus on the positive and the good memories I had of my Dad, like fishing and camping. Throwing the football in the evening as I prepared for the season. Working together and long talks as he helped me through life.

The last memory I have of my Dad was we prayed and he called for my Mom. He said "I love you Mama." She replied "I love you Pop." And they fell asleep beside each other in their bed. It was really a peaceful and beautiful end to a very stressful day, and ultimately my Dad's life on this earth.

Currently I am dealing with my Mom and her journey with Alzheimers. Again, I could choose the depressed road, but I choose to control my mindset. I have such good memories of my mama. I think of all the great food she used to make. I remember her help with my music lessons. She drove me all over the countryside for different events and groups I was in. She was always there to love me when I was down and needed a hug.

I appreciate all the time with my parents. Now, I have been able to give a little back and help them.  My Mom is in a memory care facility. I take care of her finances and the supplies she needs.  I take her to the doctor and visit her on a regular basis, sing with her and tell her I love her.  You see, I was really blessed with the time I did have with my Dad, and still have with my Mom.

I count it a blessing and an honor every moment I still have and every time I visit her, I remember it all could be gone in an instant!

## KEEPING ON

If I could give you three things that would help you, motivate you, and inspire you they would be:

1.  Live for Today

2.  Make Every moment Count

3.  Live on the Bright Side of Life

## LIVE FOR TODAY

It is good to plan and be thoughtful in our life.  As we have discussed, we need to know where we are going, but don't lose track of the moment.  You can make each moment count but you have to live for today.
Each day is precious.

## MAKE EVERY MOMENT COUNT

This moment will not come again, so what are you doing?  Remember, time is nonrefundable. How are you making the most of all
you are given?

## LIVE ON THE BRIGHT SIDE

When you have a positive attitude, you live on the bright side.  It doesn't mean everything is always going to come out rosy, but you will have a much better perspective about it,
whatever it is.

**LIVE FOR TODAY!**
**MAKE EVERY MOMENT COUNT**
**LIVE ON THE BRIGHT SIDE OF LIFE**

## CHOOSING YOUR PERSPECTIVE

Life really is all about perspective.  Life is going to happen.  The good and the bad.

Good News!  How you handle it is up to you.  Your attitude and your mindset are always yours for the choosing!  When you focus on the positive and keep a good attitude, everything seems better, even during the rough times.

I think many of us don't take time to stop and consider that we need to enjoy the life we have now because we are not guaranteed tomorrow.  We need to take advantage of every opportunity we have.  Our families and friends can be such a blessing if we let them.

Make the best of things.  Be significant in all you do and become a success in your personal life and your business.

**GO CHANGE THE WORLD!**

# 8
# *SIGNIFICANCE THAT LASTS A LIFETIME*

There was a time when I believed significance came through success and possessions.
I was determined that if I got a great job, worked hard, and made enough money all would be good.  Come to find out, that isn't necessarily true.

### *What creates significance in your life?*

This life before us is amazing, and we all strive for something.  Many strive for success measured by accomplishment and things:  A new job, bigger house, a better car, more stuff... but is this really success?  Does this really fulfill the need you have in your life?

John Maxwell puts it best ...

> *"Success is mainly about myself...*
> *Significance is mainly about others.*
> *I've known many unfulfilled successful people,*
> *but everyone I know living*
> *a life of significance is fulfilled."*

This is truly what it comes down to.  Helping show others their value will bring you significance, which in the end will make you truly successful.  But like everything else in this life, it is a Journey!

There have been many people that have been significant in my life and made a real impact by adding value to me.  As I mentioned before, Professor Ellis, my journalism professor at Oregon State University, was such a person.

## SIGNIFICANT INFLUENCE

I was in my junior year at OSU and needed a journalism class.  The class I wanted to enroll in was full, but I was told I could speak with the professor and see if she would make an exception.

I went to her office and was invited in where she gave me clear expectations for her class.  She told me she was a tough teacher, but also would provide me all the help I needed.  She explained how she structured her class and how she graded.  It was a real-world scenario.  We were writing an article for a publication and she was our editor.  We would write and she would edit.  We did this week after week.

As far as grading, if I make one error on a paper, even a punctuation error, I would drop one grade.  If I made two errors, I would drop another grade.  If I make a third error, I might as well forget a grade.  She looked at me straight in the eyes and said, if that was agreeable, she would let me into her class.  I said yes, mostly because I really needed the credits to graduate.

*BEFUDDLED?*

When I left her office, I almost collapsed.
I thought, what have I done?  I am going to
flunk this class.

Well, I learned very quickly she was true to her
word.  She was tough but she always answered
any questions and gave me all the help that
I needed.

One of the toughest aspects of her class was
typing.  The personal computer was brand new
and expensive and most of us could not afford
one.  I had to type and retype the same article
over and over as she made edits.  I was not
a good typist and having to type it again and
again increased my chances for errors.  I was
forced to slow my pace, then double and triple
check my work.  This created many late nights.

One huge plus about Professor Ellis's class was
she taught us her trick for proofreading.  It was
simple: read it backwards.  Starting at the end
and reading one word at a time out of context.
This kept you from reading over mistakes, which
we all tend to do.

As the class progressed, I found that not only
was she a tough grader, but she expected you
to come to class.  Oregon State was a large
university where most professors didn't really
care if you showed up or not.

One day I woke up late.  I had about a 7-minute drive and 5-minute walk to class.  I woke up 20 minutes before I had to be in class.  I flew out of bed, took a 1-minute shower, threw my clothes on, and drove as fast as I could to the campus parking lot and ran!  At the top of each hour there were bells that rang from the Memorial Union Building in the center of campus.  As I ran, the bells began.  I made it to the building but was about 1 minute late, rushing into the classroom and to my seat.  I can still hear Professor Ellis to this day, as she looked over at me and said, "Nice you could join us Mr. Hedge." The disappointment in her voice just killed me, and I was never late again.

What that showed me is that she cared that I was there, and that gave me great significance as I was a floundering college student still searching for where I fit into life.

What made Professor Ellis the best professor I had at Oregon State was not grading and the fear it brought to my inner being, it was her clarity and the significance she brought to my life.  She laid things out for me very clearly and then followed through.  What I did was important to her and significant.  That significance fueled me.

By the end of the term, I not only excelled in her class and received an A, I earned her respect and that gave me a sense of significance.

Oh, don't get me wrong, it was hard and took many late nights, but it was worth it. When I was stuck and didn't think I could do it, I would hear her say ...

### *"Just do the next dumb thing."*

This was one of her favorite sayings and my most memorable quote. What she meant by that was just keep going. Keep writing. It will all work out and it did.

### SIGNIFICANCE HAS THE POWER TO LAST A LIFETIME.

To this day I still can hear her voice saying ...

### *"Just do the next dumb thing."*

## SIGNIFICANCE

Professor Ellis was a significant influence in my life, and what she taught me continues to shape who I am today. It drives me and keeps me going. Her significance has lasted a lifetime.

*Who has been a significant influence in your life?*

Significance that lasts a lifetime is created by someone who invests into others, is present, and truly cares. Their actions and authenticity show their true intent and gives them a unique ability to connect and shape lives.

When you are befuddled and things don't seem to be working out, what do you do? Do you just do the next dumb thing? I think that is great advice, because if we allow ourselves to get stuck in a rut all momentum stops and we go nowhere.

I can assure you that if you use this principle in your personal life and your business, you will attain true success. You can use it to drive others to achieve great things as well. Significance and success are contagious, so keep it going! Take what you have learned from significant people in your life and spread it to others. You can be that someone for someone else.

It all starts with you. Be authentic, and don't be afraid of showing others that you're not perfect. If we try to show people we are invincible, we will fail because none of us are. When you create significance by your actions and invest in others, it adds value to you as well. When you are confident in your own skin and are outward focused, it is amazing what you can accomplish.

Ask yourself the following questions...

1.  Are you invested
    in your own significance?

2.  Are you invested
    in the significance of others?

3.  What can you do to create a true culture
    of significance in your personal
    and business life?

### ARE YOU INVESTED
### IN YOUR OWN SIGNIFICANCE?

It all starts with you and how you feel about yourself. If you are not invested in your own significance you will not find real success. If you're not invested in your own significance no one else will be either.

How do you build your own significance?
You invest in others. You need the passion, confidence, strength and clarity that comes with personal investment.

There is nothing that makes you feel better than to help someone else, make them feel significant and watch them grow into a significant person. Then they can carry on and invest in others.

### ARE YOU INVESTED
### IN THE SIGNIFICANCE OF OTHERS?

If you are not outwardly focused, helping to create significance in others, your life will be very empty and shallow. You need to love your neighbor as yourself and help them to feel significant. You can help with their process by adding value through your actions and words.

### WHAT CAN YOU DO TO CREATE A TRUE CULTURE
### OF SIGNIFICANCE IN YOUR PERSONAL
### AND BUSINESS LIFE?

This is an ongoing process of maintaining an outward focus in your life, thus creating significance all around you. It is a daily habit, very purposeful and intentional, but it can be done. It must be done if you want to create, develop, and maintain a true culture of significance.

My parents were a great example of creating significance in my life. From the time I was born, they were all about helping me grow and develop into someone that was confident and significant.

They were always encouraging me to step out and try new things. They helped me and inspired me through their actions as they were actively encouraging others.

I owe my attitude and my ability to encourage and lift people to my parents.  They gave me so much positive reinforcement that I couldn't help but pass it on to others.  I was blessed and I know not everyone has parents that invest so much into their significance, but we all have a choice.  I acknowledge it is harder for some, but it can be done.

**ARE YOU INVESTED IN
YOUR OWN SIGNIFICANCE?
ARE YOU INVESTED IN
THE SIGNIFICANCE OF OTHERS?
WHAT CAN YOU DO TO CREATE A TRUE
CULTURE OF SIGNIFICANCE IN YOUR
PERSONAL AND BUSINESS LIFE?**

## GROWING THROUGH SIGNFICANCE

I loved playing sports through school.  I was a good athlete, but I was definitely not the star.  When I began playing in elementary school, I loved basketball.  As most young boys, I dreamed of a career in the NBA.  I practiced with my Dad at home.  He even built a basketball court for me.

At first, I came off the bench and had to work to earn playing time.  A couple of the star athletes talked down to me because I was not one of them.  My Dad and Mom however encouraged me and built significance in me.  They told me I could do anything I put my mind to.  So, I began to practice more.  My Dad would work with me and I loved the time with him.

One practice, the time finally came and my coach took me aside.  He told me I had earned a spot in the starting line-up.  He said I was one of the hardest working players he had coached. I was so excited.

I went from the player who was not looked at as significant to the one full of significance because of my coach.

I grew into a person of significance because of my parents and their encouragement, help, and love as well as the encouragement of my coach by elevating me into the starting line-up.  It was a day to remember.

## MOMENTUM

Significance builds momentum.  It gives you confidence in your abilities because others reinforce you.  Because of my positive last year in elementary school, it propelled me into the following year when I entered Junior High.

I began to have much more confidence.  Not only was I a starter on my 7th grade team, I was also the leading scorer.  It was a transformation because my parents and my coach had created significance in me.  And right there beside me, as assistant coach that year was my Dad.

When I look back, I was so blessed with a great childhood. I realize not everyone is, but there is someone in your life that has been that significant influence. Use those experiences to propel you today in all that you do.

Don't make excuses just because you had a rough road. Remember, you still get to choose how you respond to the life you are given. You are truly blessed and significant.

Get out there and live a life of significance! Add value to others by giving, helping and doing! You will be rewarded daily with the joy it brings to others. There is nothing like the feeling of making someone feel significant and better about themselves. It is truly a gift that keeps on giving.

# 9

# *THE CHOICE IS YOURS*

Do we sit around watching Netflix all day, or do we get busy and make things happen? So many people today feel entitled and everything is owed to them. Unfortunately, they are still sitting on the sidelines waiting. Waiting for their ship to come in and something big to happen.

## OUT OF NOWHERE

It felt like my head exploded, but with one left hook I was staggered and fighting to stay on my feet. In an instant, I was thrown into a situation that I never wanted to be in.

I am not sure how it even started. I'm sure words were exchanged and the situation came to a boiling point. It was the summer before my sophomore year in high school. Football practice had just ended and I was walking back with the team to the locker room. Something was said and the fight broke out. Unfortunately, I was right in the middle of it.

The part I really hated about fighting, besides the pain, was that everyone else just circled up and cheered it on.

The truth was I was a lover not a fighter, so I was not prepared at all and I was definitely not prepared for the left hook across my jaw. Sam, the boy who hit me, was smaller than me but had been a boxing champion in Alaska before he moved to Oregon.

In an instant, I had a choice to make.

Since I was not a boxer, but was bigger than him, I did what my Dad had taught me and put him in a headlock.  The good part was it kept him from punching me anymore, but it pretty much put things at a standstill.

Well it all ended, as most fights do.  When I got home, I was a mess.  My Dad told me to go back that night and face the situation head on.  So, that is what I did.  By that evening at practice it was all but forgotten.  In fact, Sam and I went on to be friends for many years.  All the way through college.

## UNEXPECTED CHOICES

When the unexpected happens, you have a choice.  Do you hit the situation head on or do we retreat?   The choice is yours.

It really can't be overstated, where you choose to go with what life throws at you determines your ultimate path.

I love the verse in the 34th chapter of Psalms that says ...

> *"Taste and see that the Lord is good.*
> *Oh, the joys of those who take refuge in Him."*

Taste and see means you have to try, take action, and choose. God blesses that. Your life will be filled with joy and fulfillment if you choose the positive path.

It took me years, but the Lord finally got me on the right path!

What you see in people is sometimes deceiving. Many people seem to have it easy and all together, while others seemingly struggle at every turn. What we assume to be true, usually isn't because we don't know what goes on behind the scenes, below the surface of what people are willing to share.

***So, what are you going to do when life throws things at you?***

## ROLL WITH THE PUNCHES

I have worked for several companies over the years. I have always had the itch to try something on my own, but have never had the courage.

Then came Covid 19!

I had started my coaching, consulting, and motivational speaking business on the side but wasn't really going anywhere with it. Suddenly my life changed.

*BEFUDDLED?*

Suddenly God created space for me to try something new.  I made the decision to go full time helping people through inspirational coaching, consulting, and motivational speaking. I teach people how to network and connect, building community and driving great prospects to their business.

There is always the fear factor when launching out on your own, but I decided now was the time.  I felt God directing me to do my real passion in life, and that is working with people, helping them to achieve their dreams and living their best life now!

Now is a time like no other because we are in the middle of the Covid 19 Pandemic and everyone seems to be in a state of befuddlement and chaos in their life.  Now more than ever we need a voice for calm, peace, and kindness.  We need to build communities in our personal life and business to combat the loneliness and isolation that has been thrust on us by this virus.

There is no magical pot at the end of the rainbow.  Life doesn't come together all by itself. God put us here with a plan to make things happen!

When it comes down to it, the choice is yours! No matter what is happening around you, you control how you react to it.

Just like Chuck Swindoll said ...

> **"Life is 10% of what happens to us and
> 90% of how we react to it!"**

As I've stated before... be an actor not a reactor! It is one of my favorite quotes. We need to go on the offense, not just sit back and wait for it to come to you! Remember, you have the power over you!

*So where are you in life right now?*
*Are you doing what you want?*
*If not, what do you really want to do?*

## MINDSET

Things could be going badly all around you, or you could be on top of the mountain of success, I do not know. My guess is that most people are somewhere in the middle. Good days and bad days. But the question is what do you do with those days?

Today you need to evaluate how you look at the world. Your mindset is up to you. The choice is yours. You cannot control other people, and you cannot control what goes on in the world around you, but you can control what you do.

**DO YOU WANT TO SUCCEED
IN YOUR LIFE AND BUSINESS?
WELL THEN DO IT!**

Success doesn't always mean money and things, sometimes your contribution will be making things better for others.  In fact, giving is one of the surefire ways to have significant and true success.

### WHEN WE GIVE, WE RECEIVE.
### THAT IS A SUREFIRE PRINCIPLE OF LIFE.

Some of us are blessed with giving and helping as part of our daily job.  I believe when possible, this is always the best way to live.  Doing a job you love and helping others at the same time.

Every day we wake up we have a choice.

### *Are we going to take full advantage of our day?*

Life is filled with choices
each and every moment.

I remember back to my high school graduation. My plan was to go to college.  I had chosen the University of Oregon and was accepted and heading there with my best friend.  Everything seemed set, and then came a big life decision.

## CHANGING DIRECTIONS

My music director pulled me aside and said there were tryouts at Oregon State University for vocal scholarships and he felt that this was a better choice for me.  He believed they had a

better music department and I should
give it a try.

I decided to take a look and audition.  He drove
me there one cool Oregon Saturday morning.
Things went well and I was offered the
scholarship.  Now I had a big decision to make.

I chose to make the change, and my best friend
and I quickly applied to OSU and were accepted,
and the rest is history.  Not only did I change the
direction of my life, I also changed the direction
of my best friend's life.

That one decision affected the entire direction
of my life and set the course for where
I am today.

I have never regretted my decision.
I learned a lot at Oregon State.  Not just from
class, but from my involvement in the social
part of college.

Choices are an integral part of life and we have
to continue to move forward and choose.  Not
be paralyzed by fear, but find peace in our life
and realize we will occasionally make mistakes,
but as we discussed before, that is just a part of
our learning process.

There are several things you should consider
each day as similar choices come your way.  You
need to evaluate where you are, where you are
going, and how you are going to get there.

*BEFUDDLED?*

Here are five things you should consider.

1. Are you at peace?

2. Are you motivated?

3. Are you living your plan today?

4. What are your overall objectives?

5. Will your objectives get you where you want to go?

### ARE YOU AT PEACE?

Are you at peace with your current situation? It all starts with where you are currently. Do you have a peaceful mindset or are you constantly befuddled?

Are you currently living a life of contentment? By this I don't mean you don't want to improve and move to the next level, but as Paul says in the letter to the Philipians ...

### *"I have learned to be content in all circumstances."*

When you are content but not satisfied, that is a good place to be. It keeps you moving and driving to be better, but gives you peace each step along the way.

### ARE YOU MOTIVATED?

Do you have the drive to move forward and do great things?  Are you motivated to move to the next level while being at peace with yourself?

Motivation can come in many ways but no matter what motivates you, you can use it to drive you to the next level.  You have to love what you do to be truly motivated to succeed and not just survive.

### ARE YOU LIVING YOUR PLAN TODAY?

You have to start with a plan and then live the plan.  It is no good without action.  Start living today and you will move forward, even if you make some bad choices along the way.  Just keep moving.

Remember, failure is inevitable and that is ok. That is how you learn and grow as you are living you plant today.

### WHAT ARE YOUR OVERALL OBJECTIVES?

Where are you heading?  What are your overall objectives?  With a clarity of purpose, great things are possible.  So decide what your life objectives are and start moving.

To reach your overall objectives you must know your "Why" and have goals for what you want to achieve.  When you have a sense of direction it will help you focus on your objectives.  With the focus you can make a significant impact on life.

### *WILL YOUR OBJECTIVES GET YOU WHERE YOU WANT TO GO?*

Will your objectives get you where you want to go?  Are they really yours?

Don't live someone else's dream.  You get to choose your path, so make it all yours!

Don't let others, including your family or friends, tell you what you have to do.  You get to choose. If you try living someone else's life, you will get off track and never be content.

Your path in life depends on you and your choices.  No one else.  Focus on today and set out to be you and live your life!  So, remember to ask yourself these questions.  With the answers, you will be on your way!

**ARE YOU AT PEACE?**
**ARE YOU MOTIVATED?**
**ARE YOU LIVING YOUR PLAN TODAY?**
**WHAT ARE YOUR OVERALL OBJECTIVES?**
**WILL YOUR OBJECTIVES GET YOU WHERE YOU WANT TO GO?**

# 10
# *LIVE THE LIFE YOU CHOOSE*

Life was simpler years ago.

I grew up in Oregon City, Oregon, a small suburb of Portland.  It seemed like everybody knew each other and everyone was connected naturally.  I had a great life and loved every moment of my childhood.

I was sure that my Dad and Mom knew everyone because they were involved in everything.  This may not have been totally true, but that's the way I felt and it felt good.

My parents were creatures of habit, like many of us, and always went to the same places.  I have come to learn that the reason they did was because of their connections they had made.

We went to the local Chevron service station for gas because we knew Marv the owner. Mom and Dad took us to Tradewell, the local grocery store, because we knew Betty the checker.  Dad and I had our hair cut at the local barbershop because we knew Ed the barber. We had so many connections and my folks were comfortable and wanted to support the local businesses and the people they knew.

*BEFUDDLED?*

This was my life.  A simple life.  We knew each other, worked together in harmony, and helped each other.  There was more clarity in life and we were definitely less befuddled.

I yearn for that simpler life again.  This is the life I want to live.  I want to be so connected and care about my community and have them care for me.  I want to be in it together like we used to be.

We have become so disconnected over the past several years.  A Pew Research Center Report from August of 2019 says 80% of adults 18 to 29 don't really know their neighbors and are definitely not connected with them.

Google has replaced asking for directions and gathering information by talking to our friends and neighbors.  It is all right at our fingertips.  Another Pew Research Center Report from July of 2019 says 8 in 10 adults are online daily.  Many of us are permanently connected to our phones and computers.

We are over connected online and under connected in real life!

We get so much merchandise online today, many of us don't even know the local merchants in our town.  Amazon Prime, FedEx, and UPS trucks flood my neighborhood daily.  We have lost our connection to our local community.

Young adults like the millennial generation yearn for community. They are looking for authentic connection and true community.

***What are you looking for?***

You have the power to change and to reconnect and Live the Life You Choose!
It's really up to you!

## POWER TO CHOOSE

I am not against the ease of online and technology. But it becomes a problem when it totally replaces good old connection, friendship, and speaking with our neighbors and community.

Building a community online should not be the only community we are focused on.
We need to get back to enjoying our family and our local community.

One of my favorite activities is peaceful walks with my beautiful wife Leah. Often it is just around our neighborhood, but I especially like walking by nearby rivers or the ocean. It is just so peaceful and refreshing.

In just the past couple of weeks we went to the Oregon Coast with our daughter Kyla and walked on the beach along the ocean. It is so calming and definitely the life I choose.

*BEFUDDLED?*

Sometimes we take our trusty beagle Maddie, because she loves to walk.  She gets so excited!

Just yesterday, we went up along the Santiam River, with Maddie, to a place called Fishermen's Bend and walked along the river and took some pictures.  It was a gorgeous day!

These are the moments I live for.  This is the life I choose.  Leah and I make time for these moments because they are a chance to spend time together; spend time in God's creation; rest and recalibrate; and enjoy our journey together!

You have the power over your life choices.  You choose how you deal with all life throws at you. Maybe recalibrating and taking a peaceful walk is what you need.

When it is all said and done, your life is really made up of your choices.  Sure, there are outside forces that may cause you to pivot and go another direction, or maybe you have to recover from some challenging circumstances, but ultimately you choose what you do with what happens to you.

Some may think that is over simplistic, but it is really true.  Life happens and then we make choices about what to do with it.  Both good and bad, and everything in between.

## CHOOSING WHAT'S IMPORTANT

My favorite choices in my life revolve around my family.  We always took one or two family vacations per year.  We were able to go to places all over the country as well as Canada and the Caribbean Islands.

The choice to do things together as a family was always so rewarding.  We explored Oregon together, took the subway all over New York, visited Disneyland in California and Disney World in Florida!  We visited Alaska and saw glaciers, and Hawaii and snorkeled and saw beautiful colorful fish!  We sailed the Caribbean and explored the water with stingrays and swam the coral reef with a shark.

Once we took a vacation in my Mother-in-law's and Father-in-law's motorhome and went from Oregon, through Idaho, into Wyoming and Yellowstone Park, up into Montana, over to South Dakota and visited Mt. Rushmore.  We came back through Colorado and Utah, and back to Oregon.  It was a wonderful trip.

We also once flew to Washington DC and drove up the east coast.  We got to stop in Philadelphia, Gettysburg, New York, and Boston. It was so much fun!

Choices can make memories or choices can bring challenges, but whatever life throws at you, take it and use it for good. A chance to celebrate, or a chance to learn and grow.

So here are four things you can remember when life happens:

1. Only You Can Choose Your Actions

2. Choices are driven by Attitude

3. You Have the Power Over You

4. Your Choice Can Make It A Great Life

### ONLY YOU CAN CHOOSE YOUR ACTIONS

You are in charge of you. We cannot control much in this world, but we do have the power to control our actions.

Actions are driven by your attitude and it is so important to intentionally develop a positive outlook. If you keep a positive attitude then your paradigm will be much brighter and your actions will reflect that paradigm.

### CHOICES ARE DRIVEN BY ATTITUDE

The attitude you choose drives your choices because it is your baseline for decision making. As I just stated, your attitude will bring much more positive actions.

With a positive attitude comes a positive outlook which drives positive actions.

### YOU HAVE THE POWER OVER YOU

There are some pretty crazy things that happen around us. Just look at where we are currently with Covid 19 and the cultural battles. We cannot control all the circumstances and people around us, but we do have the power over how we respond.

We have the power over our actions and how you choose to be, in spite of all the things happening around us.

### YOUR CHOICE CAN MAKE IT A GREAT LIFE

Because we are ruled by our choices, we have the choice to make it a great life or not.

Is your glass half empty or half full? I choose overflowing! I choose to make it the best life I can. I get excited because I get to choose!

*So, what is your choice?*
*Do you want a great life?*
*What is your endgame?*

I truly am excited each day I wake up, because I know there is so much possibility ahead. I have a chance to learn and grow; a chance to live and add value to people; a chance to encourage someone and make someone smile!

**Life is good!**

So how do you want your story to end?
Or better yet, how do you want
your day to be today?

**ONLY YOU CAN CHOOSE YOUR ACTIONS
CHOICES ARE DRIVEN BY ATTITUDE
YOU HAVE THE POWER OVER YOU
YOUR CHOICE CAN MAKE IT A GREAT LIFE**

## HERE WE GO!

Fight through the noise.  Be intentional.  Find purpose in the midst of the chaos.  Plan the moment.  Don't live beyond now.  Failure can be built on.  Life is precious and it can be gone in an instant.  Create significance that lasts a lifetime.  The choice is yours.

**LIVE THE LIFE YOU CHOOSE!**

You can do it... Make it an Awesome Life!
It's Your Choice!!

# *CONCLUSION*

***What are your goals for your life?***
***Where are you now?***
***Where do you want to be?***

I have a friend that once gave me an excellent way to rid yourself of problems and challenges.

Write your problems and challenges down on a piece of paper.  What is Befuddling you and distracting you from the goodness of life?

After you write it down, rip it up and throw it away, and let the problems go with it.  If you are a visual person like me, just watch as all the problems go and then choose to release them.

Next, make a promise to yourself that you are going to form good habits to rid yourself of all that you wrote.  It is up to you and you get to choose what you do.

## SO, DO IT!

Crazy you say... it can't be done!  How do you know until you try?  Sure, there may be bumps in the road, and you might not accomplish all you set out to do, but you will definitely improve your life and how you look at all that comes your way.

## MAKE IT AN AWESOME LIFE... I DARE YOU!

*"Choose today whom you will serve...*
*as for me and my family,*
*we will serve the Lord."*

**RUSS... AKA #RUSSSELFIE OUT!**

# *NOTES & QUOTES*

## CHAPTER 1

Gary Keller with Jay Papasan, "The OneThing: The surprisingly Simple Truth Behind Extraordinary Results" (Bard Press, 2013)

Ed Mylett, "#Maxout Your Life" (Mylett Communications, 2018)

Steven Curtis Chapman, "More to this life," (Sparrow Records 1989)

Joyce Meyer, "PsychologyTomorrow.com" September 29, 2016

Chuck Swindoll, 90/10 "The Grace Awakening: Believing in Grace Is One Thing. Living It Is Another" (Thomas Nelson, 2010)

## CHAPTER 2

Dave Ramsey Quote (DaveRamsey.com)

John Maxwell Quote (johnmaxwell.com)

Bob Goff, "Love Does: Discover a Secretly Incredible Life in an Ordinary World" (Nelson Books, 2012)

## CHAPTER 3

John Maxwell Quote (johnmaxwell.com)

## CHAPTER 4

Chris Carey (www.chriscarey.vision/blog May 2, 2019)

Leah Hedge, "No Regrets" (No Regrets CD, 2003)

## CHAPTER 6

Bob Goff, "Love Does: Discover a Secretly Incredible Life in an Ordinary World" (Nelson Books, 2012)

John Maxwell "Failing Forward: Turning Mistakes Into Stepping Stones for Success (Thomas Nelson, 2000)

John Maxwell, (JohnMaxwell.com)

Simon Sinek, (Twitter @simonsinek)

John Maxwell, (Facebook, @JohnCMaxwell)

## CHAPTER 8

John Maxwell, "The Power of Five: For Network Marketing," John Maxwell Company, 2019)

# *AUTHOR*

Russ Hedge is a positive force in today's busy, hectic, and often negative business environment. He is a master connector, working in marketing and sales for over 30 years.

He has been recognized as a Top Salesperson in multiple industries for his skills in Networking and Connecting! He is also a licensed minister and has served in worship ministry for over 30 years.

Russ loves to encourage, inspire, and make people smile. He has been married to his beautiful wife Leah for almost 33 years and has 2 adult children Kyla and Connor, and a daughter-in-law, Gabby.

His goal is to add value to people by encouraging and helping them to live a more engaged and positive life. Russ lives each day with a positive attitude and is passionate about life.

Russ is available for one on one coaching, consulting, or motivational speaking events. He is here for groups looking to be inspired and move forward in life with a positive attitude and gain an adventurous spirit!

Check out his website at www.russhedge.com and schedule time to chat, or contact Russ today at russ@russhedge.com.

Also, check out his video/podcast "Marketing with Russ... aka #RussSelfie," available on YouTube, Facebook, LinkedIn, and most podcast platforms.